Skyfighters of France

Captain Guynemer

Skyfighters of France

An account of the French War in the Air
during the First World War

Henry Farré

LEONAUR

Skyfighters of France
An account of the French War in the Air
during the First World War
by Henry Farré

First published under the titles
Skyfighters of France

Leonaur is an imprint
of Oakpast Ltd

ISBN: 978-1-84677-786-8 (hardcover)
ISBN: 978-1-84677-785-1 (softcover)

http://www.leonaur.com

Contents

Introduction

By

CAPTAIN HEURTAUX CAPTAIN DE KERILLIS

CAPTAIN ROECKEL

LIEUTENANT PARTRIDGE

1

October 27 (1917)

Dear Chief:

I am very much behind in writing to you, and I hope you will excuse my long silence. I have just gone through a very trying time and have suffered much with my wounds, owing to supervening complications. Now I am finally able to pull through and somewhat re-established in health, and I am attempting to make up for lost time.

You have asked me for a story of a fight in the air, and I am going to narrate one of my latest experiences, although it is not of a very recent date. You know that I had no sooner returned to the front than I was again wounded.

We had just arrived in a new locality. The first days were passed in arranging our hangars, and particularly in very carefully overhauling our machines, which had considerably run down during our long period of activity.

On several occasions already, the Boches had been flying over our heads, taking advantage of our forced inaction. From the ground we could distinguish their black crosses, not without cursing our inability to pursue them. Finally, the machines were ready; it was beautiful weather—not a cloud in the sky. A strong wind was blowing but it was at least favourable for an excursion against the enemy. I had great hopes, therefore, of being able to give him battle and to return without being too much knocked up.

Everything was carefully straightened out on board. I got in and was trying the motor when suddenly some white tufts appeared over our heads, and in their midst—a plane; no doubt about it; it was an enemy, arriving just at the proper time.

I let go in all haste, without losing sight of the bursting shells which gave me my proper course. I went up as rapidly as possible; the motor worked beautifully, so I could soon make out my enemy. It was without question a reconnoitring plane, flying around over its objective, taking photographs. So much the better! In that case the observer would be less likely to notice my presence.

I tried out the machine gun and tested all my instruments for the last time, as I had arrived in the danger zone. Everything was going well, and all I had to do was to begin the fight.

The Boche was about eight hundred yards off—seven hundred yards yet to run before opening fire. I approached him rapidly; a few little white clouds appeared in front of me; I was discovered. The gunner had already commenced firing; it looked as if the fight would be a hot one, and I began zigzagging at once, so as to destroy his aim. The little white tufts were growing farther and farther away; all was well. Our distance apart diminished more and more.

The machine-gun volleys now lasted longer, a good sign that the enemy was getting excited. We still drew together, and I could make out clearly the shapes of the pilot and passenger; but I saw I must get closer. Finally I could see the face of the machine-gunner very clearly. I was at good range, and it was now my turn to reply. At the first shot the Boche commenced to fire, then to dive more and more.

The two machine guns rattled away without pause, and the enemy tried in vain to escape, until after some sharp turns his machine suddenly began to descend—the pilot must have been shot—and this manoeuvre of his brought me very suddenly into his arc of fire. A few shots—sudden noises around me—a violent blow in the left leg—am I wounded? I shake myself, but can't discover anything; I am flooded with water, with gasoline; a sudden moment of fear—shall I take fire? No smoke, thank God!

And now what had become of my adversary? These few seconds had given him time to take a fresh position. My motor stopped; how should I be able to continue the fight? Luck followed me, however; the Boche at once began to turn his nose down. I flew in his wake, joined him, and so took up a most beautiful commanding position.

Again I commenced firing at him, never letting him go. We fell vertically, going like mad. The machine gun crackled incessantly, but the enemy never replied. Finally my ammunition gave out; I had to abandon my prize.

It was now high time to think of myself and to select a landing-place, not an easy thing to find in this hilly region. I finally discovered a little strip of land close to a wood; it was the only possible place. The high wind allowed me to come to earth slowly in the midst of holes and logs, which I finally did without accident. I jumped out of my machine in haste, and found it in a very sad condition, indeed, completely unfit for service. As for me, some shots had gone through my teddy bear. I was fully repaid by my adventure.

A little while later, an automobile picked me up and took me back to camp. There I found—with much pleasure—that my German had fallen within our lines, and was still burning on the ground. I went to look at the wreck, and that same night started out to look for a new machine which would allow me to begin again.

Goodbye, my dear Chief. I hope that luck will favour us and that we may soon see each other again. I send you a cordial handshake.

Heurtaux

2

Why do we Bombard?

March 9, 1917

To bring home to the Boches the anguish, the suffering, and the sorrow of war; to make their sufferings like our own; to avenge our women, our innocent children assassinated by them—to kill, to kill many!

To paralyse their industrial life; to quench the life of their factories; to strike the workman at the anvil; to strike terror into their workshops; to block them in the air—to destroy, always to destroy!

To reduce their aerial force; to dominate them in an attack; to hold them on the defensive; to fight them and to conquer them at home; to have the mastery of the air, their air and ours—to strike without ceasing!

Why do we bombard?

In order to save ourselves.

Why do we bombard?

So that in their ruined towns, they also shall remember!

De Kerillis

3

July 31, 1917

My dear Farré:

You have asked me for something on army corps aviation, and more especially on aviation in connection with the control of artillery fire. I am going to give you, as far as I am able, all I know about this in a few words.

As a general rule, people know nothing about this class of aviation work. Whatever may be the special employment of the aviator, be it fire-control, photography, bombarding, or reconnaissance work, he is invariably asked these questions: Have you brought down your Boche? How many Boches have you brought down? Where is your *Croix de Guerre*? The knowledge of most people is limited to those questions.

As to the simple fighter, who is a spectator every day of the

work of planes of every kind, he sees them—these gallant fire-control planes—right over him and not very high up either, proceeding easily and in all tranquillity, seemingly moored to the particular patch of ground over which they are working; but this regular going and coming becomes very monotonous to the onlooker.

It requires a little pursuit plane—swift and handy to bear down on them, to place them in the limelight. Sometimes a few shots of 105's, bursting at the height of these control planes, will lend a little interest to the scene, and the spectator amuses himself by following their slow evolutions in and out in the midst of those small black-and-white tufts of smoke. He guesses the point at which the next shell will be placed, and watches to see how close it will burst to the plane, and this affords him a considerable amount of interest.

But what matters it to those who are high in the air, what the interest is of those watching them from the earth! Of what interest is it to them, when shells are bursting, which every now and then come close and burst even within the range of the wings of the machine! They see nothing but the little patch of earth to which they are anchored. The chasing plane looks toward heaven; he forgets the earth and that which is passing on the face of it.

The army corps plane looks toward the earth; he looks at the game like the artilleryman, and he controls it. He is the only one who takes it in at a glance. He knows so well his own corner of ploughed ground—trenches, roads, and pits—that he considers it his own special part of the earth. He is proud of his duty, and it is just pride; like a god, he commands the lightning and projects it from his batteries to whatever point he will. There are three things on the ground that must attract his attention:

1. The antennae of the T.S.F. who listens to him, replies to him, and interrogates him with the help of great white panels.

2. The battery for which he is working (strictly speaking, he should not bother himself about it).

3. The point of aim—whether it is a trench, a battery, or a shelter—his will for destruction concentrates upon that.

Whether our artillerymen fire too slowly, whether the special enemy batteries are firing too quickly for him, he is never discouraged; he must attain his end, and he does not fail.

Is his work finished? The fire-control plane comes tranquilly back to the aviation field; the pilot reports a few shot-holes in the wings, and the observer makes his report.

Pilot   N   Observer   N

Concentrated Battery X upon such a point; observed effective fall of shot; three shot-holes in the machine.

And that is all. They have nothing further to say of the work; they begin again on the morrow, and again on the day after the morrow, and so on forever, unless surprised in the midst of their work by some enemy chasing plane, or—struck by a 105—the gallant plane finds, one day, a glorious end.

If the end only appears glorious to the vulgar, you can understand that those who fly may well be proud during their lifetime of the greatness of their role—so proud that they may indeed care little for the opinion of others.

I am happy, my dear Farré, if I have given you, in this letter, not only a look-in on fire-control aviation, but a little of the sentiment of its modesty and at the same time of its importance.

Please feel assured that this class of aviation will indeed contribute its full share to the next great success in which it shall take part. In this happy hope, I beg you to accept my very cordial regards.

                                                        Roeckel

4

                                                October 3, 1917

My dear Chief:

What is my opinion in regard to bombarding? I can explain it by saying only that, from the very first trial of this method, I have devoted myself to it entirely; and as the attraction is so strong, I shall be only too glad to give you my ideas concerning it and the principles which have convinced me of its value.

From the very beginning, bombarding by aeroplanes offered to me a strong attraction by reason of its apparently unlimited destructive power. After the early experimental period was over, you will remember our great raids of 1915, which confirmed a success made possible by tentative effort in this direction. This side of aviation is most captivating, the source of impressions which it is impossible to feel in any other branch of the service.

The great beauty of a departure at sunrise; the evolutions of the little flotilla; then the crossing of the lines and the heading to the east; no more trenches, no more impassable wall; one flies to the enemy, seeking him at rest.

Lorraine—the Vosges—Alsace—the Rhine, and then—Germany. The factories first feel the destructive force of the planes; then the cities beyond the Rhine—in order to avenge the German lust and the innocent victims of our unfortified cities—then no weak hesitation.

The danger may increase—but what is the difference! With that feeling of absolute detachment from terrestrial things; the spirit free, and without care of bullet or gun, they steer straight to the end in view, drinking in all the beauties of the voyage, and enjoying the ideal sensations to which it gives birth, in anticipation of a perfect accomplishment of the mission in hand.

That is the wonderful part of bombarding aviation—attractive from its heroic side and captivating from the impressions it produces; but it is closely linked with another function of war which is even more intimately in touch with battle, and that is night bombardment.

Let us consider the field of activity in this. In modern warfare an immense amount of material is constantly used up and destroyed, and means must be taken to keep an ample supply in the rear, to be drawn upon as necessary for the troops in the trenches; at the same time it must be out of reach of enemy guns. The artillery has made great progress in this, by increasing the range of their guns and consequently their radius of action, but even then the reserves and material cannot be reached by their cannon. This hammering by enemy guns can only be efficient in the front zone, so that fresh reserves and new material must constantly be brought up.

So this is the business of night bombarding squadrons: to harass the enemy, strike his reserves, cut his lines of communication, set fire to his railroad stations and his aviation hangars, blow up his ammunition depots, fly over his cantonments and bivouacs, flood them with projectiles, decimate the adversary, and deprive him of rest; as a result, on the following day at the hour of attack, we shall find only demoralized troops, without supplies. Between times during fine clear nights, we carry the action farther away. The ammunition factories, foundries, and forges receive a visit from our planes, and a giant charge will result in putting out of use for long months the factories attacked. Still farther, there will be sometimes reprisal raids on the large German cities on the other side of the Rhine.

For these different objects there must be a corresponding means of execution, varying according to the nature of the mission. The light and fast plane will strike the cities which are industrial centres, which distance makes almost invulnerable; and the fighting plane—a big machine—strongly armed, can attack all organizations at the front as well as the factories in the rear. In fine, the conditions of adaptation of these planes vary every time, according to the requirements demanded by the proposed objective.

If it is desired to cut lines of communication and interrupt traffic, especially large bombs are dropped from a low altitude and these throw the railroad into such confusion as to require long days of repair. An entire squadron passing over such a place will make such a road totally impassable; or again, it may be individual attacks on running trains followed by derailments, fires, and the stopping of all traffic.

Is it desired to destroy ammunition stations? This is a new class of operations; to cover the entire surface of the depot with a great number of small shells, and accomplish its certain destruction by explosion of the shells close to the projectile heaps. On an aerodrome the same tactics are employed, but with incendiary shells, or a few shells of large calibre dropped from a very low height directly upon the hangars. If reserves are seen to be coming, it is necessary to use special shells which burst into an infinite number of pieces (shrapnel), followed by grenades and machine-gun attacks on troops at the disembarking pier, or farther out on the road leading up to their final positions. Furthermore, machinery of factories cannot escape wrecking from an attack of high-power projectiles dropped upon them.

The diversity of these expeditions, the varying circumstances—always new—in which they are conducted, induce a feeling of fresh interest upon the occasion of every sortie, and offer opportunity to study the methods used, with a view to approaching constantly nearer perfection. It is a strong stimulant for the natural-born bombarder, whose real vocation it is, and who interests himself in his task because conscious of its great power.

How wonderful are the sensations felt in these night flights over the field of battle; lighted by its thousand fuse lights, bursting shells, and the lines of fire of the machine guns; you will remember, dear chief, having tasted something of this in the great days of Verdun, 1916, where you took part with us in the operations of that time.

It is a spectacle of sublime and savage beauty this—to view a field of carnage by night. When the lines are passed and one engages, in his turn, in the great struggle, surrounded by the illuminating rockets, in the midst of bursting shells, crossed by the searchlight beams searching the heavens with its rays, and to extinguish it with a salvo from a machine gun—to do this without being blinded—then one feels an indescribable joy.

When the end is in sight and the precise moment approaches when the projectiles are to be dropped, one realizes at once the amount of danger that had to be overcome in order to succeed; the fascination of firing, and finally that feeling of strong domination, of superiority over an enemy that one holds at his mercy, and that with a simple turn of the hand he can destroy or save. Such realization awakens the recollection of days gone before, and thrills one with joy in the work of destruction.

An immense field of development opens up before a man in bombarding aviation, and through that, will finally come success. It is a real arm of offense, and carries the war into the enemy's country. Daily and nightly our colours cross the Rhine and presage the next great victory.

Partridge

CHAPTER 1

The Storm Breaks

At the windows of the Plaza Hotel at Buenos Aires, my soul oppressed with infinite anguish, I awaited news of the war. *Dieu*, is it possible that there is a man in this world capable of taking such a responsibility? "No doubt," I murmured, "the Kaiser is capable of anything." I remembered his speeches, his acts, and I recalled his persistent efforts devoted entirely to the increase of his military forces both on land and on sea; the intimidation which he attempted on all peoples; his amiability to those whose neutrality he thought he could secure; all that I believed had been done with but one end in view—domination in war. For ten years past, such a termination appeared to me inevitable; France, of course, was always the most menaced, but my dear country, devoted to liberty and peace, constantly repelled that bitter cup.

While I thus reflected, I saw a long and solid mass coming down Florida Street towards the hotel. An intense heat, upon which the freshness of the night had no effect, hung over the city like a fog of fire. The shouts of the crowd reached my ears, muffled and mellowed through the heavy atmosphere. I ran downstairs and saw below in the lobby a polyglot mob assembled. My worst suspicions were realized; people avoided one another, some with shame written in their faces. Germans were talking amongst themselves in low voices, evidently suppressing an ill-concealed joy. I read their thoughts! They were mostly business men or brokers, happy to see the great day arrive at last.

17

War was declared with Russia, and France was allowed twenty-four hours to affirm her neutrality, but within that time, Germany had already thrown her forces into France and invaded heroic Belgium.

I made up my mind at once, and decided to take passage on the first boat leaving port. But the ocean was not safe, not yet free of German cruisers, and I was obliged to wait fifteen days in the Argentine capital. There the people, almost to a man, shuddered with undisguised horror and hate of the Germans. The bankers alone, who were almost all Boches, remained indifferent to these public manifestations, which one could see came straight from the heart.

Crowds were massed constantly before the newspaper offices, hungry for news, following with interest the opening moves of the gigantic struggle about to commence. One paper, the *Prensa*, had planted a powerful searchlight on its roof and indicated by coloured beams the ebb and flow of victory in the initial battles. The beams were red for Boche and green for us—green for Hope! The crowds were so great that the mounted police were often obliged to press them back.

The entrance of England into the war was received with frenzied joy, and that night all who were recognized as Englishmen were carried in triumph on the shoulders of the crowd, and if at that moment Argentina had followed the wishes of her people, she would have been early an ally at our side, even before Brazil.

The day of departure arrived at last, and the consul handed me a secret letter of instructions. The boat on which I had taken passage was the finest one of a French line that had ever anchored in this port, and was called *Lutetia*. By the irony of chance, it was moored along-side of a German boat of the newest design, the *Cape Trafalgar*, and a heavy cable held them together.

Twenty-four hours previously the *Cape Trafalgar* had weighed anchor, for what reason her officers alone knew; certainly it was not to escort us to France. There was nothing aboard her but guns, and there was every indication that she would transform

18

herself into a pirate. The *Lutetia* was fully loaded with provisions of all kinds and an amount of treasure; in addition, there were about two thousand army reservists and some women and children.

The captain of the *Cape Trafalgar* must have chuckled to himself. He was a disgustingly gross person, whose face was as red as his hair. Closing my eyes I can see this human monster lapping his thick lips with his tongue, which formed a disgusting break in his unkempt beard, his squinting eyes and the thing called a smile, which deformed his filthy mouth. In my daydreams I can see this human carrion, drunk with champagne, insult, bind, strip, and violate the women and children; throw them overboard to the accompaniment of the wild bursts of laughter of a crew who had lost the qualification of human beings, to kill without trace, in accordance with the instructions given at a later date by the Count de Luxbourg, the German Minister to the Argentine.

The captain of the *Lutetia* decided to wait forty-eight hours, so two days later we sailed from Buenos Aires, and at nightfall we anchored in Montevideo Roads. We had not yet left neutral waters, and anticipating no danger of attack from the *Cape Trafalgar*, we continued our course to the entrance of the bay, the *Trafalgar* saluting us as we passed. She remained at anchor for four days awaiting news of our departure, and the morning of the fifth day she disappeared. That evening at five o'clock we weighed anchor and sympathetic Montevideo gave us a hearty send-off'.

Orders were issued on board to dine early, and to show no lights after dark; so that at night the ship was in complete darkness; the lights of the cigarettes and the cigars of the smokers being the only precaution against collision. But there was no joy fore-and-aft, and each one asked himself if he would live to see the morrow. Few passengers slept that night. At last we saw the first ray of dawn upon the horizon—we were alone upon the waters. I learned later from the captain that we had passed quietly between the *Trafalgar* and the light cruiser *Emden*.

Lieutenant Henry Farré,

We steered a course that only sailing ships take to make an offing. Wireless messages asking constantly "Where is the *Lutetia*?" were received by our operator, but the *Lutetia* made no reply, and so we sailed on as far as the Portuguese island of St. Vincent, near the coast of Africa. The coaling port was a French Dakar possession, but the captain believed that stopping at Dakar was dangerous and decided not to coal there. Future events proved that he was right.

Here at last we received the war news of the last twenty days. The English consul, as soon as he came on board, gave us a full account of it, and handed us a complete file of his wireless dispatches. Two million Germans are at Compiègne, he told us. Consternation was painted on the faces of all, and without any accompanying news, we were unable to explain the presence of the enemy so near Paris without having fought a great battle.

"We will get there too late," said some.

"It could not have happened," said others, and I was among the latter.

"Have any Boche cruisers signalled you?" we asked.

"Oh, yes," said he, "yesterday, at Dakar, the cruiser *Wilhelm der Grosse*—Boum!"—and he made a sign like someone throwing something overboard.

We knew then that this ship awaited our arrival, but unhappily for her, twenty-four hours too soon, for instead of meeting the *Lutetia*, it was an English cruiser she met, which showed her no mercy. A little later, the *Cape Trafalgar* met the same fate.

During the trip from St. Vincent to Bordeaux, which we hardly expected to make without adventure, we fell in with a few sail which gave us goose-flesh until our nationality was ascertained by them. At last Bordeaux and France! The steamer now ascended the green and flower-bordered banks of the Gironde, and loud hurrahs greeted the new reinforcements as we disembarked.

The battle which saved the world was in its last phase. The next day the word victory—a great victory—ran from mouth to mouth, and on the night of the 7th of September, the enemy retreated in disorder and the victory of the Marne stopped forever the invading advance of the Hun. Attila, with despair in his soul, turned his horse's bridle away from the coveted prize—Paris—which lay almost within his grasp, and which passed beyond his reach forever. The world was saved and civilization breathed again. Our army, worn out with seven days and seven nights of fighting, ceased pursuit at Soissons and Rheims, and it was then a race to the coast, to Calais; the battle-front automatically established itself in a line reaching from Alsace to the Yser.

The next day after my arrival, I was promptly at the recruiting office, but there they told me: "You are not yet called; return to your home in Paris and wait." Paris—oh, sadness—empty, silent as a body without a soul, wreckage everywhere, misery attending the improvident, the air heavy with anger and bitterness against the invader.

Tired of waiting to be called, I asked one of my friends, a colonel, to do something for me.

"But, my dear sir," said he, "you have only to keep still, for you cannot move when you are at the call of the Minister of War."

"But can I not anticipate the call?"

"I suppose so," he rejoined; "come and see me tomorrow and bring your *livret militaire*" (army descriptive list).

The next day I became a soldier; my friend had got me admitted into a quartermasters' company. I was not long in recognizing the fact that I was *embusqué* (shelved). My captain, whom I asked every day to allow me to accompany him to the front, invariably told me to wait, that my turn would soon arrive.

It did come at last, but not through him. My friend, Do-Hu, captain aviator, dead on the field of honour a year later, but then just returned from Indo-China, where he had been on duty, came to see me and said brusquely, "What are you doing here?"

"Don't you see that I am *embusqué* and that I am laid off? Can't you take me away with you?"

"What shall I do with you?"

"Whatever you wish."

"But you are too old for flying."

"My dear man," I said, "you cannot make me believe that you have only pilots in your formations. There are other things necessary; and then again you might form with Commandant de Goys a bombardment group which would suit me exactly. The principal thing for me now is to get out of this Paradise. Do you need an orderly?"

"Oh, very well," said he, "if you must go, give me some paper and I will write a request to the Governor, General Galieni. His chief clerk is one of my friends, and will take the matter up promptly."

The result was, the next day I was the orderly of Captain Do-Hu, but not for long, I must admit. The captain whom I left did not wish to lose me, and it was necessary to obtain his signature almost by force. As I got ready to leave, the General of Division Niox, governor of the Invalides, and director of the Army Museum, called me into his office and said to me, "I am directed by the Minister of War, in agreement with the quartermaster general, to create a group of artist-painters, whose duty it will be to paint certain phases of action, so as to immortalize on canvas true pictures of fighting in the field. Do you wish to join it?"

"General, I am certainly delighted that you honour me with your choice, but since yesterday I have belonged to an aviation formation" (though I took care not to add that I had begun as an orderly).

"*Eh, bien, c'est parfait*; I had not thought of the fifth weapon. Would you like to be a painter of aviation?"

"Willingly, General. You may count upon my enthusiasm for that kind of work."

From that time on, I was an aviation-painter and an orderly for Captain Do-Hu.

"I am leaving," said Do-Hu to me. "Arrange your affairs and join me when you can. We have a fine future before us, and I hope you will find plenty of new and fascinating work, so that your talent can develop. Regarding Commandant de Goys, he

THE AUTHOR'S CARD OF IDENTIFICATION AS AN ARTIST

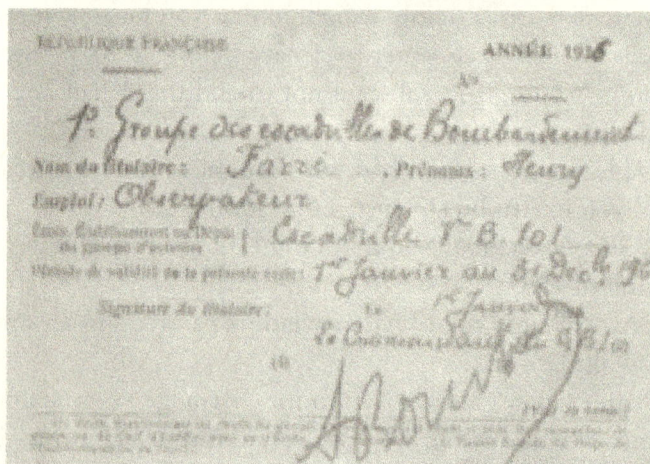

THE AUTHOR'S CARD OF IDENTIFICATION AS AN OBSERVER IN THE
FIRST GROUP OF BOMBING SQUADRONS

will probably bring you with him."

And so I started. First, I wish to give you a brief idea of our state of preparedness.

It is no longer necessary to prove to the world how little France desired the war. A good army existed, but there was nothing behind it in the way of supplies; no heavy artillery, or at least very little of it. Some old worn-out types of guns remained; our seventy-five millimetre gun alone demonstrated its superiority and still demonstrates it. And to that, to the courage of our soldiers, and to the genius of our chiefs are due the victory of the Marne, the greatest among all great victories.

Aviation, though born in France, did not exist—so to speak—as compared with the present day. Each army corps had its squadron, and trials had been made at the great manoeuvres; but the chiefs did not believe in its utility, and sad experience was necessary to convince them of its value. Six months after the beginning of hostilities, there were still chiefs who were ready to deny its usefulness, although victory never could have been obtained without the flyers.

Modern arms are so murderous that unless combatants are willing to be annihilated, they must hide under ground, or dig themselves into trenches. Armies engage now at a distance of several kilometres, artillery playing the principal role; and how can they quickly ascertain the effect of fire without the information received from the flyer? He alone can tell, because he is able to fly over the enemy lines and report the situation and formation. He can report the fall of projectiles, photograph the terrain, correct the fire of the artillery, and furnish promptly news of the enemy's movements.

In every way the supremacy of the air is necessary to efficiency. During an offensive, no enemy plane should be allowed to rise; the adversary should be kept blind, subject to the fire of artillery, without power to reply effectively. I will explain later the different uses of aviation, such as observation, bombardment, photography, fire-control, and combat.

The control of the air once obtained, the defence of the enemy, however strong, can soon be destroyed by artillery of every calibre. The infantry then may with little loss take and occupy the enemy's position, and such a result, obtained on a large front, is certain to end in the retreat of an adversary, if his reserves do not arrive in time. Thanks to our bombarding planes, a retreat can easily be converted into complete disaster.

Consider a Boche army forced to retreat. Think of the enormous amount of material accumulated upon his front since the beginning of the war; imagine the interminable convoy columns of all kinds strung out along the roads; three or four tractors disabled at the head of these columns would result in stopping the supply trains for several hours. What pleasure then would our planes have, whether of the bombarding or machine-gun type, in attacking by every means these convoys of material and human cohorts!

But to accomplish this, it is necessary to be masters of the air, and a real aerial army of planes will be required. It will be necessary from the beginning of an engagement that the air should be rid of every hostile airship, and this advantage must be retained until victory is assured. During this time, our airships of observation and of fire-control (*réglage*) must fulfil to the limit their mission of controlling the fire of the artillery. Here is the principal objective.

Our allies in the United States have found the key of victory in aviation, and I can well believe that the American pilots, of whom report speaks so well, are predestined by their skill in athletics, their tenacity, and their courage to accomplish great feats worthy of our best air heroes. The celebrated *Lafayette Escadrille*, which ranks the highest among our squadrons, will show them the way. In comparing our present-day aviation with that which existed at the beginning of hostilities, it is apparent that the progress has been astonishing. Some squadrons composed of types like Voisin, Caudron, Farman, Marane, Nieuport, were all that existed; the Voisin and Farman planes almost alone did the aviation work at the beginning of hostilities. The strong Voisin, made of metal, defies any temperature. Rain, snow, wind, and frost leave it unharmed; it requires no hangar, and well for it that it does not, for at that time there were none!

How many times at sunrise I have seen them brush the snow off these planes; seen the arched wings leave the earth and soar up to their mission! A simple tent, anchored to the ground, protected them during the night; and watchmen mounted guard over them to see that the wind did not blow them down.

It is a real war—here today, there tomorrow. Today one has a good bed and tomorrow he is satisfied to crawl under the wings of a plane for protection. Of course, one may not always have a bathroom at hand, but I am sure that is about the only thing missing. All material, all personnel are now comfortably sheltered, but in a war of advance, doubtless this comfort would be very much diminished.

CHAPTER 2

Aviation

Our aviation has become an organization of enormous importance; I cannot quote figures, but I know that in spite of our heavy production both of planes and of pilots, we do not yet have control of the air, but it is absolutely necessary for us to have that.

Directly behind our front, a great number of squadrons are detailed to be ready for instant call. They are constantly in motion and render such wonderful work that they cannot help but arouse the enthusiasm of all American aviators, and it is to these brave men that I dedicate this sketch. It is my aim to let them know in a simple way what we have accomplished in aviation in these three years of war.

In December, 1914, I left Paris in company with Commandant de Goys, who had just been appointed Commandant of the First Bombing Squadron. The nucleus of this squadron consisted of the Twenty-first Squadron V.B. (*Voisin de Bombardement*), and we were to join these two squadrons at Dunkerque, where the defeat of the Boche had already begun. We made this trip quickly and comfortably in a one hundred horse-power Bentz machine.

My heart was sad as we passed for the first time and got our first sight of the cities and towns destroyed by the barbarian. What wanton destruction! And to what end!

Having arrived at St. Pol in Ternoise, about thirty kilometres from Dunkerque, we saw in a ploughed field on the edge of the road, and in which there were a few light tractors, a dozen Voisin planes. "Why, those are my squadrons!" said the Commandant. "Stop!" he shouted to himself, for he forgot he was his own pilot. They were in fact our own squadrons, which had received instructions from General Headquarters to post themselves there and await orders.

The bombing squadron was created as an independent unit, and was intended to operate over the whole front, under orders received direct from General Headquarters. A sudden call would send us flying from one end of the front to the other on special service, to succour a defence, to make a retaliation raid on enemy manufacturing plants, or on their convoys or concentration camps. "You have been named by General Niox to paint aerial warfare! You will see some splendid work, for it is our prerogative to be in the most fascinating and thrilling places."

The officers of the two squadrons. Lieutenants Mouchard, Féquant, de Clerck, de la Morlaix, Do-Hu, and Lieutenant de Vaisseau de Laborde, Adjutants Jumel and Neurdin, and Corporal Bounier de Neufville, all veterans of aviation, were our senior pilots; and all of them, too, were noted for their wonderful prowess and skill.

It happened on this occasion that the rain came down in torrents and the only possible shelter—the one bit of dry ground to be had—was the little spots beneath the wings of the machines. The blue-gray planes shed the water like ducks, and the engines, still hot from their trip through space, instantly converted into steam the water which fell upon them.

"My dear man," said the commandant after having introduced me to all the officers, "do the best you can and bestir yourself to find a place to sleep. I am going over to that *château* where Do-Hu is waiting. He has promised that there will be a room for me."

"Very well, Commandant," I said, "don't worry about me."

It was raining still, and got dark here at five o'clock in the afternoon. The little town of St. Pol was three kilometres away. When I finally arrived at the outskirts, wet to the skin, I saw a lantern waving in front of me, which sent a cheering ray through the darkness, and I was able to see the shapes of two *poilus* wearing goatskins, and looking like anything but soldiers.

I heard the challenge, "Who goes there?" and a bayonet was thrust at me.

"France," I answered. The man with the lantern drew near. I gave him the password.

"All right, go ahead."

"Surely," I said to myself, "only a Gascon would have such a brogue."

St. Pol happened to be at this time ten kilometres back of the enemy's lines. The houses used nothing but candles and oil lamps; and the streets were littered with all sorts of vehicles and filled with people running into one another.

It was still raining. "Well, this is fierce," I said to myself. "I'll be hanged if I can find a lodging-place here." I went into what they called a hotel, and found it crowded to capacity. "Can you give me something to eat?"

"Oh, yes," the proprietor said. "I still have some beans, and if you can't get a room, you can always sleep in the stable."

"All right," I said; "I'll eat first, and then I'll try the sleeping accommodations."

"The dining-room is over here, sir."

I found the dining-room full to overflowing; it was about ten yards square and lighted by four oil lamps; there was such a fog of tobacco smoke within that I could almost cut it with a knife, and it was fully a minute before my eyes could distinguish anything through it. My throat was choked, and I felt that one must be very hungry, indeed, to stand such an atmosphere, in which the brawn and sinew of the land was concealed in the muddy cloaks of the young soldiers.

There were about one hundred of them massed in the room, and it was the first time that I found myself face to face with that simple but heroic figure—the *poilu*. They were there in force, and so covered with mud that it was difficult to distinguish the colour of the uniform they wore.

Alongside of me, seated at a table, were four Algerian machine-gunners, one a Parisian and one a Gascon, and they came to the rescue.

"Come on, sit down," they said, offering me the end of a bench.

"Well, my friends, how goes it?"

"Fine; it's a little damp, but that makes no difference—on *les aura!*"

"Ah! Those dirty dogs," said his companion. "There were two of them hovering over a trench this morning, and I certainly sent them both to hell; I gave it to them strong enough anyway."

"Don't flatter yourself, old chap, those two wretches that you shot have been dead for three weeks, and have been hanging on the barbed wire in front of my sector ever since."

"That can't be; I saw them fall."

"So, then it was your shot that cut the barbed wire?"

These *poilus*, almost without exception, belong to the plain people, for the most part peasants, but they were full of eagerness and enthusiasm, in spite of the hardships they suffered. They had been hardened in the trenches, but at this early period of the war the trenches were very hastily made, and no one ever remained in them long. I certainly admired these men, assembled from the four corners of France, and I wish I could adequately describe the stoicism of these honest souls, but I cannot—it was truly sublime. They suffered everything, the enemy's fire, fatigue, dirt, discomfort, cold, hunger, often getting their supper late, and passing entire nights in the rain up to their knees in water. Happily enough, all that is now over.—But I am getting away from my subject, which is aviation.

At nine o'clock the lights were put out and everybody looked for a place to rest; all was quiet. As for myself—like Jupiter changed to a bull—I went into the stable and lay down beside a cow. At times, I felt its hot breath warming my stiffened limbs, and my pillow of straw seemed very soft. O weariness, you are sometimes welcome and offer sweet recompense! The heavy bombardment at the front did not prevent me from falling fast asleep.

The sound of loud reports at dawn, which turned out to be enemy planes leaving their calling cards, woke me from a deep sleep. I rubbed my sides, and cramped and lame from my night's rest on that spring-less bed of straw, finished my toilet by dipping my head in a bucket of ice water which was probably intended for the animals to drink, and then went out.

A pale, cold sun shed its feeble light; in the streets there were mixed groups; African *Spahis*, wearing their beautiful red cloaks, stalked about on foot or rode on horseback among ammunition carriages, guns, and vehicles of every kind.

Our Headquarters was close by, so I paid my respects to General de Maudhuy, commanding the army, and a few minutes later I got to the flying-field, which might be called anything else.

Lieutenant Mouchard, who was known to be a very brave man,—at times almost reckless,—took me under his wing, and I at once became a member of the First Squadron, First Group of Bombarding Planes; a squadron celebrated throughout the army for the number and variety of its successful exploits. After five minutes' conversation, we found ourselves mutually pleased with each other.

"It is very strange," he said to me, "I feel as if I had known you for years."

As a matter of fact, I had the same feeling in regard to him,—a deep and mutual liking sprang up between us, and as the reader will see later on, it was a liking which endured to the day of his death.

For an hour or more we talked of flying, and I asked him to tell me the story of his squadron, which was V.B. 114, now become, under the new grouping, V.B. 101.

"It is extremely interesting," said he, "but unfortunately, I have never taken any notes. We did some fine work—those old busses certainly have a story to tell of the retreat of the Marne; with orders and counter-orders, they didn't know which way to turn, but one thing is certain, we killed an enormous number of Boches.

"What a pleasure to see a convoy on the march! We would straddle the column at a good height—about a thousand meters—so as not to be reached by the bullets of the infantry (*fantassin*), and then the bombs fell! Sometimes one of these, well placed, meant one hundred of the wretches laid low.

"The horses would scatter, the ammunition wagons would capsize, and then those terrible arrows (*fléchettes*) would follow—five hundred at a time. It was a veritable rain of iron of a most remarkable and wonderful penetration. Sometimes a horseman and his horse were pierced through and through; men fell like flies without a sound and without any wound, apparently.

"Later on, the Boches made and used them, and had the insolence to cut on their side the following inscription: 'French invention made in Germany.'

"Afterwards I brought two of them from Nancy, that fell about three yards from me; I could hardly pull them out of the ground, they had gone so deeply into the soil of the road; they bore this inscription and the date, 1916."

"How about aeroplane fights?"

"Oh, absolutely absurd! No one ever dreamed of fighting; an enemy flyer, a prisoner, once told me that, and added, 'Why fight? Don't you find your duty sufficiently hazardous, and isn't it foolish to try and make it more so?'

"Of course," Lieutenant Mouchard went on, "flyers saluted each other as they passed on their mission, but that practice did not continue very long. The revolver, which they carried in case of being forced down within the enemy's lines, was at first the only weapon that flyers had; it was that or nothing. Later, followed the short musket (*le mousqueton*), which was hardly more effective, but it had the advantage of greater precision and of carrying farther. The first plane brought down with one of them was a Boche, and to Lieutenant Frantz, in a Voisin plane, fell that honour. Afterwards, we were armed with one machine gun; soon after, with two, and later on, some planes carried small cannon.

"Come on, let us join the squadron," he said.

I was deeply interested in this life which was so new to me; it was the first time I had been to the front, and as a member of a squadron too! Notwithstanding my gray beard, which seemed to surprise the machinists, I considered myself a good rookie.

We started the engines; the machinists adjusted them, while others tried them out. Across the road there was a racing-field studded with a dozen little wooden houses painted white.

"What do you think of those dandy little houses as dressing-rooms in which to don our teddy bears?" said Mouchard to de la Morlaix.

"Impossible, my boy, they have no mirror; give me my tractor."

"Well, for my part, they'll serve very nicely as a dry place to stand in. I'll try them," said Mouchard; "and so much the worse for the racing club of St. Pol."

"What do you want, Dominique?" said Mouchard, turning to his chauffeur, and taking a package from him; "what is this?"

"I don't know, sir; an orderly of the General Staff gave it to me."

The address read: "Lieutenant Mouchard, Commandant of the 101st Squadron, V.B."

"Well, that's odd—no stamp—where did this come from, and what is the idea of this cloth wrapping two yards long?"

He took it off, and found it to be coloured red, white, and black, and beneath the wrapping he found a linen bag like those in which peasants stow away their savings—it was full of sand.

"Don't you understand?" said de la Morlaix.

"No, not yet; do you?"

"I think it is a message a Boche plane has dropped; rip open the bag; there may be a letter."

As a matter of fact, on shaking the bag, a letter fell out.

"What can this possibly be? read the signature—'Sergeant Barrès'"

"So it's Barrès," cried Mouchard, glancing over it quickly. "He 's a prisoner."

34

"Is that so? Give me his letter—let me read it," said de Clerck impatiently.

After a pause, Mouchard read in a loud voice:

My dear Lieutenant, my dear Friends:
During our last flight, the stalling of the motors obliged us to land in enemy country. Up to the last, we hoped to be able to repair the damage, but unfortunately were discovered before we could do so, and found ourselves surrounded on all sides by soldiers firing on us, in spite of our signs of surrender.
We fired our machines and succeeded in running the gauntlet of musketry and in surrendering to officer aviators, who came to our relief and stopped all further attack. I must testify to their gallant attitude towards us, and I wish to thank them now for having afforded us a means to communicate with you.
We deeply feel our bad luck, and we think of you and of our dear France, which our captivity will prevent us from serving with all the ardour we possess. However, we know we have always done our duty,
and we beg you to please notify our families.
Here's to you, and long live France!
                                        Sergeant Barrès.
P. S. From the chief of the enemy squadron. Ask the lieutenant commanding the 101st Squadron V.B. to let us know what became of our two flyers who fell within your lines on
the —— at ——
                        With thanks,
        signed —— Commandant of Squadron No. ——

"Well," said de Clerck, "they're pretty decent."

"Oh," replied de la Morlaix, "it is to their own interest. Are you going to answer them, Mouchard?"

"Yes, I think I will, but without saying anything to the commandant, for communicating with the enemy without his permission is absolutely forbidden."

Suddenly, a smile lighted up his face.

"I am going to answer them, for I know the flyers they are asking about, and tomorrow, if the weather permits, I am going to send them what they want by way of the air, but it will be a reply *à la gauloise*. I tell you what, Farré, get a sheet of paper and make a sketch to illustrate my letter, a sketch to impress them with our high morale and our love of fighting."

A moment later the drawing appeared.

"There, Mouchard, how do you like that?" I said.

"Great, splendid!"

At the top of a page I had drawn a superb French rooster crowing victory, and at his feet sprawled a dying German eagle, gripped in the Gallic bird's claws.

"Make him say something pleasant, so as to give them an extra dose to swallow," said Mouchard. "Oh, I have an idea—quick—give me your pencil," and seizing the pencil, he wrote an interpretation of the rooster's crow as follows: "Salute, old man, here's to our next meeting!"

Then we made a little linen bag, put in the letter and sketch, and wrapped it in a tricolour pennant. He let the message fall the next day within the enemy's lines. That shows how little hatred existed at the beginning of the war between enemy aviators, but I am compelled to add that this kind of courtesy did not last long.

During the day Captain de Marniez, Chief of Aeronautics, came to see us.

"Will you come with me to the front?" he asked.

"Willingly, Captain."

"Have you been there yet?"

"No, Captain."

"Then this will be your baptism of fire?"

"Yes, Captain."

"All right, shall we start? We will visit artillery headquarters, and get the instructions for the start tomorrow."

As we went along, the artillery fire became more intense and we were soon within range.

"These shells that fall around us now are the reply to that battery of 155's over there, in the middle of that little bunch of make-believe trees," said de Marniez to me; "in five minutes, we will be there ourselves."

We were passing a village when a shell fell just behind our car, struck a house, and blew off the roof.

"They are firing on the village," said the captain.

The chauffeur, who was not keen to catch the next shot, speeded up. Two batteries of 155's were hid under some transplanted trees, screened from the eyes of the Boche aviators. Not far from the guns themselves some holes had been dug in the ground, one for ammunition and the others for shelter in time of great danger. At this moment a long whistle passed over my head.

"What is that?" I asked.

"That's a shell in flight; but never fear, that one, at least, is not for us."

I turned and saw a large cloud of yellow smoke marking the fall of the shot about three hundred yards away. Our guns kept up a constant fire without regard to the enemy's fire. Suddenly, at the blast of a whistle from the chief of the piece, the crew all ran for the shelters. One shell struck very close, but, fortunately for the captain and myself, did not explode, for neither of us had been able to get away.

"Such is fate," said the captain to me.

"True enough," I replied.

"Nevertheless, as we have to stay here another half-hour, let's get behind that haystack. It 's absurd to expose ourselves when we don't have to."

And so it was in this wise that I received my baptism of fire— on solid ground, I mean,—not in the air.

CHAPTER 3

My First Flight

The first aviation group remained only eight days at St. Pol; the expected attack did not occur, and we received orders to proceed to the camp of Châlons. The planes weighed anchor and sailed away through the air, while I followed the tractors in an automobile.

The little village of Mourmelon is situated on the outskirts of the huge field of Châlons, where formerly the same Huns, led by Attila, were wont to say that not a blade of grass should ever grow where their horses' feet had trod—a striking analogy to the modern Attila. One can still see here such remains of old fortifications as time has left behind, and they exactly resemble our modern trenches.

This place awakened in me recollections of youth. It was here, twenty-five years ago, I finished my apprenticeship in the artillery, but the little village since then had grown to a small city, and few things remained of former days; among them, however, was an inn which was dear to us.

The field was covered with barracks; one division had its staff there. In peace-times, it was used as an aviation school with big hangars, and all paraphernalia was installed that was necessary to aviation. However, the Boches must have known of our arrival, for a short time afterwards, they bombarded our hangars; a few men were killed and a few planes destroyed.

Here, for the first time, I went up in an aeroplane. It was a beautiful winter afternoon, and the sky was almost cloudless.

Lieutenant de Clerck was sent on a special mission of observation over the enemy's lines. A massing of troops had been reported in the rear of these lines, and the Staff wanted information of this movement.

"Is it cold up there?" I asked of de Clerck.

"No; go as you are, but take a helmet," he said. The motor started; we headed up into the wind and after going a hundred yards, we took the air. At first, I did not notice that we were flying; it was only after looking down and seeing the houses become smaller and smaller, and disappear under me, that I really felt that I had left the earth behind.

The higher our plane mounted, the more the panorama expanded and the view widened. The line of the horizon followed our ascension, and remained, very naturally, always on a level with the eye. We had reached an altitude of about fifteen hundred yards; a ceiling of clouds stretched out just above our heads. All at once I noticed a burst of black smoke appear upon an immaculately white cloud; then another, and after that, three or four more; they were about three hundred yards from us and appreciably much higher.

"What's that?" I inquired of de Clerck.

"That is the Boche; those are Boche cannon shots."

"Is that so! Well, I don't consider that very alarming."

"Just wait," said he with a wave of his hand.

As we crossed the enemy lines, the Boche artillery saluted our passage and the puffs were much nearer, as the gunners had rectified their aim. One shell burst quite close, and shook us up a bit. The burstings made my ears sing, but the old engine ran on regularly—unscathed—only our wings had been touched.

"They are starting something," said the pilot to me.

"I should say they were," I replied. "Is this going to keep up?"

"No; five minutes more and we shall be out of this."

As a matter of fact, not long afterwards we entered a thick bank of cloud. For a time that seemed to me interminable, I could see nothing around me but clouds. I had the sensation of

DESTRUCTION OF DRACHEN BALLOONS

sailing along within a sphere of infinitely light white cotton; my feelings I cannot describe.

"Let us turn back, I want to see it once more."

"No, old man, don't forget we have a mission—we haven't the time."

The plane now nosed down through an opening about over our position of observation. We had just accomplished our mission, when fresh cannon shots reminded me that we belonged to this world. The gunners did their best to bring us down, but a hospitable cloud hid us from their fury, and protected by that we got away and regained our lines, still wrapt in the dream of the last few minutes. The oscillations of the plane called me back to life. I looked at my pilot and noticed that he was writing.

"Look here, what are you doing?" I said.

"I am writing to my wife," he replied.

"That's a fine state of affairs; and what about the plane?"

"Don't worry—it knows what to do."

I observed his movements carefully, and I saw that occasionally touching the tiller with his knees, he steered the plane at will. Ten minutes afterwards, by a clever spiral, we came to earth at our point of departure. Our flight had lasted two hours.

De Clerck got out and I tried to do the same—impossible; my feet would not bear me.

"Will it be necessary to get a derrick to get you out?" he said.

"I shouldn't wonder; I think my feet must be frozen."

I felt a frightful reaction—I laughed, I cried, but all the same I was able to get myself out without assistance. I suffered all that day; without regret, however, for I had felt and seen the most beautiful among the experiences of the air. It was the first time since the beginning of the war that our planes had not slept in the open. Commandant de Goys seemed well pleased.

"We're better off here, and it's a shame that the Boche can bombard us, for he will make it lively for us."

As a matter of fact, three new shell-holes not far from our hut were proof of the insecurity. Eight days later we made our presence felt in several bombarding raids on their communications. Profiting by the darkness of night, they brought up trains armed with artillery, and severely bombarded our camp; we did not give them time to rectify their aim, and the first thing next morning we left for Verdun.

CHAPTER 4

Night Flying

We were not to remain very long, either, in Verdun. We lodged in a handsome house next to the cathedral, and our planes, too, found a warm and dry housing in the aviation camp within that strongly fortified area.

We had come there to check the audacity of the Boche flyers, who often came to bombard the city. Three days after our arrival, a telephone message from Staff Headquarters told us that a squadron of hostile planes was crossing our lines in the direction of Verdun. There was a general hustle to clear for action. The machine guns were installed on the machines and five planes got away at once.

The enemy planes were already in sight, and soon came under fire of our artillery, but passing through its barrage fire they arrived over the city. During all this time our own planes were mounting higher and higher and nearing the enemy; bombs fell, heavy explosions shook the air, often followed by loud crashes. They aimed at the cathedral, and one bomb fell between that and our hotel. Its heavy wooden door was already pierced through and through by the fire of the five enemy planes; four of them had retreated; the fifth, having dropped to the rear, was joined by one of our planes and the battle began: ta ta ta ta ta ta ta ta.

The planes replied in rhythm and soon the Boche lurched side-ways and fell in Deaumont Wood, pierced by the branches of the trees. We hastened in an automobile to the rescue of the pilots, but it was impossible to get near them, for the enemy, knowing our sense of fair play, were certain that some rescuers would gather at the point of fall of the plane, and in order to kill us, concentrated on that spot a rain of projectiles.

We had to wait until nightfall in order to rescue the two flyers, who were only wounded. They were carried to the hospital, and one of them—the son of the director of the military school of Danzig, M. X.—succumbed to his wounds. His *carnet de route* showed his brutality and his odious conduct towards women, and he was buried without military honours. The other, the pilot, in spite of his serious condition got well.

The next day we tried to interview him; his name was X—— and he was the first pilot who had bombarded Paris.

"And the Zeppelins—why do they not come to Paris?"

"The Zeppelins are not for Paris; they are for the British."

A flame lighted his dull eye; he had fully expressed his sentiments in regard to Great Britain, and his head falling back on his pillow, we ceased to question him.

"Goodbye, old man," said Mouchard, who had brought him down, in English.

After this raid, so unfortunate for the Boches, Verdun was left in peace.

The first group was then sent to Camp de Mellette at Châlons-sur-Marne, where we suffered our first bereavement, for Lieutenant Mouchard and Sergeant Maillard there met their death.

Two big houses were located near our aviation field and all the officers found a home there. The mechanics slept in a tent with the other personnel. The group was unexpectedly increased by a third member; the Third Squadron V.B. 103, commanded by the gallant Captain Benoit, came to join us at Camp de Mellette. Here the first group really began its career.

The enemy's lines were scarcely fifteen kilometres away, and we went up every day. Nothing kept us from going except rain. There were no hangars, and the planes were always out in the wet or snow; they were strongly built and could stand anything. Some pilots—notably Lieutenant de Vaisseau de Laborde, Mou-

44

chard, de Clerck, and de la Morlaix—bombarded the lines as much as three times a day.

Luncheon brought us all together in the big dining-room, where a fire of green wood almost suffocated us with its smoke. The conversation was always animated, each one describing his flight.

"Oh, those beasts certainly gave it to me," said de Clerck; "what a mess I was in—five shell-holes in my machine and my pump broken. The dogs are progressing, for at one time I did not know where to turn; there were shells bursting all around me. How they hung on! They never left me until after I had passed our lines."

"With me it was different," said Lieutenant de Vaisseau de Laborde; "that cursed Do-Hu with his mania for prowling about did not lead me down a path of roses."

"How was that?" I asked.

"This is how it was," replied Lieutenant de Vaisseau de Laborde; "we were in full range of the heavy shells, and I saw them pass humming over my head like big black flies. I knew that if one ever touched my plane, it would be goodnight. Of course Do-Hu insisted on pushing on, but when he saw these shells he stopped insisting. Isn't that so, Do-Hu?"

"So you say," said Do-Hu.

In the evening we all scattered. Châlons, the only important town within ten kilometres, extended its hospitality, and whether to make purchases, or for other reasons, not all the mess were always present at dinner, which was a soft thing for the mess caterer, for every one absent or late paid a fine of three francs or else a bottle of Bordeaux. It was always jovial and gay with us.

And what was I doing all this time? I flew sometimes and took part in certain flights, for I had my mission as an artist to accomplish, besides my military duties. I was all ears when my comrades told their adventures, and all eyes when in the air. Of course, being only a student observer, I was picking my way and training my eye. Now, instead of seeing things horizontally, I saw them vertically; that is to say, up and down.

45

Three months had passed since my arrival, and I did not yet apprehend all the pleasure I was to have by seeing things with my transformed vision—my eye and brain were not yet accustomed to it. The Commandant told me not to get depressed, that it would come in time; and it did come shortly afterwards.

The weather turned rainy, and strangely enough, if it rained during the day, the night was always clear—a terrible disappointment to Mouchard.

"Don't you think it's rotten to have bad weather all day and fine weather at night?" he said upon his return from Châlons. "I simply must fly at night, and believe me, if my mechanic is there, I'll begin tonight, as it is bright moonlight. I can get away all right, but it's the landing that bothers me. I have an idea; three torches will be enough to light my landing-place. Dominique, stop at the *Escadrille* and call my mechanic," he said to his chauffeur.

A moment later his motor was humming, and passing in front of his torches, he flew off into the dark, and soon I no longer heard the noise of his engine overhead. Fifteen minutes later he landed again without accident.

"Old man, it's wonderful up there—not a breath of air; it's simply ideal to fly at this time. The visibility is good; at first one sees nothing, and then gradually the eye becomes accustomed to the half darkness and the roads can be distinctly seen. Of course, tonight the moon is especially bright. Tomorrow I will mention it to the Commandant."

We entered the house in high spirits, where there was great excitement, and those who had gone to bed got up again.

"I say, Mouchard," asked de la Morlaix, "did you hear that plane that flew over our field?"

"I should say I did, for it was I!"

"Is that so? Really, old man, I congratulate you; and how did you like it?"

"It is the ideal time for night bombardment, and if the weather continues good, imagine how we can surprise those brilliantly lighted Boche cantonments!"

Enthusiasm was at its height and everybody wanted to go. So it was on that very night, that night bombardment was first tried, which later opened the way to so many acts of heroism. The next day at roll-call, Commandant de Goys called Mouchard.

"Well, Mouchard, it appears you gave a nocturnal exhibition last night. I heard you, and I said to myself, 'Who is the fool doing those stunts?'"

"Yes, sir, it was I, and I now request permission officially to do it over again."

"No; but really do you think that—"

"I do, sir, and by taking proper precautions, I am free to say that in fine weather it is quite possible to conduct night bombardment."

"Very well, come in and see me this afternoon and we will organize for this evening; the moon will be pretty fair, and let us hope it will be clear."

"Well, Mouchard, are you going to do it over again tonight?" said de Clerck.

"Yes, old chap, if the weather holds."

"Would you mind if I made a trial flight beforehand?"

"Not at all, though you 're crazy to want to do it."

After dinner he took me by the arm. "Come on, Farré, let's go over to the Commandant's; there should be a naval officer there who has charge of the searchlight signals. The Commandant is waiting for us."

"Is it all right, Mouchard?" said the Commandant, "and is the weather good?"

"Splendid, sir; one could read a newspaper by the light of the moon."

"All right; join your squadron and have everything in readiness in half an hour."

We went out; the moon was beautiful, there was no breeze, and the air was very mild for the month of March. When we reached Squadron Headquarters, the searchlight was ready to make the signals agreed upon.

De Clerck, with de Boisdeffre as observer, was making his

first try. Shortly after the arrival of the Commandant, de Clerck landed. Approaching Mouchard, he whispered to him, "Look here, the weather is changing up there; there is a heavy humidity which may change into anything."

"Really?"

"Yes, be careful."

"Very well, old man."

"Are you ready, Mouchard?"

"Yes, sir, I only want to change two spark plugs which are broken, and I will be ready."

I asked him timidly to take me with him.

"You must be crazy," Mouchard replied. He went into his tent, which served him also as an office.

"Maillard," he cried (Maillard was his sergeant observer), "put on your flying rig, for you are coming with me."

"Very well, sir," answered Maillard without hesitation.

He was so much loved and so admired that anyone would have died for him without a thought.

They got into their machine; the engine was purring along regularly; its noise and the sparks it shot out into the night made it look like an infernal machine. He gave it the gas, the mechanics cast off the moorings, and the plane shot out into the dark at a speed of sixty kilometres an hour. Very soon it left the earth and disappeared from view, the noise of the motor being the only indication of its location. A small pocket lamp that he lighted from time to time gave us his exact position.

During this time the moon was being covered with a veil; already some drops of rain began falling, and I thought of the warning of de Clerck.

"Let us hope that he comes down in time, for if he doesn't, and is lost in the mist, he will not see the torches that mark his landing-place, and he will surely be killed."

The noise of the motor grew less and less—they had left us; my heart was saddened; I felt their going as sorely as if they were never to return to us. I could hear nothing now. The night was black—there was no moon, and snow had begun to fall. "Oh," I murmured, "they are surely lost."

I peered towards the horizon, and suddenly, about five kilometres away, I caught a light which looked like a shooting star falling to earth at an angle of about forty-five degrees, and suddenly a great light filled the air. Petrified, I grasped the arm of Captain Mache, who was near me.

"He has just fallen—look there—his machine is burning."

"No—it isn't possible."

"Who can it be, then? We no longer hear the noise of his motor."

Without another word he jumped into his automobile and darted off at full speed towards the light, followed by his companions. Alas!—it was he. As quickly as possible we put out the fire which enveloped their bodies, at great risk of burning ourselves; we dragged them from the smoking debris of the machine, which was completely destroyed, and they remained there stretched on the ground—both of them—lighted tragically by the flames bursting from the gasoline tank.

General Boue, commanding an army corps, who was passing at the time, arrived on the scene before us, and standing uncovered, he saluted the two heroes who had died in the defence of their country. We were stunned and unable to rid our minds of this heroic tragedy. The colours painted on the machine were spared by the fire, and stood out in all their glory and symbolic purity. The snow was falling fast now, and seemed to be weeping at this sight of earthly woe.

The parlour of the castle was turned into a funeral chapel; the two coffins—side by side—were watched over by two officers until the hour of burial. During the obsequies, and while the ceremony was in progress, three machines flew overhead, rendering the supreme honours. The two heroes rest in the cemetery of Lepine, in the shadow of the wonderful Gothic church which the Boche had spared—no one knows why; and not far from there a large oak cross in the open field marks the place of their fall. A week afterwards the first group left Mellette, and all the machines, as they flew away, dropped flowers on their comrades' graves.

CHAPTER 5

On the Road to Nancy

A superb day, with a radiant sun and dusty white roads. The evening before, the commandant had received orders to leave, and to be at Toul, about kilometres from Châlons, in the course of the afternoon of the following day.

The night was passed in preparation; all material was loaded into the tractors, and at ten o'clock the last of them had gone. The convoy took the same road and the planes followed in the air. I could not go in a plane, as the pilots under these circumstances always take with them their machinists, in case of stalling. At four o'clock in the afternoon the entire group was united once more on the aviation field of the fortified camp at Toul.

The commandant was disgusted, and he was not the only one; our group was far too cramped here; the field was entirely too small.

"It is not possible to remain here," he said. "I am going to telephone for us to keep on to Nancy, as that is our proper place, and the Plateau of Malzeville, whose situation for our work could not be better, is not occupied just now. From there we can attack in all directions the principal Boche towns; and especially as they expect us to bombard them and revenge Paris, they should certainly give us that place."

Of course all were agreed about the Plateau of Malzeville, because it was near Nancy, a delightful town with a hospitable and charming population, and they would certainly enjoy it.

"Do you know Nancy?" said the commandant.

"Yes, it's a bully place," I replied.

At eight o'clock in the evening the decision of the quarter-master general had been made, and preparations were under way for the morrow.

Nancy was only twenty-five kilometres from Toul. The planes received the order to leave first, and in order that they should not waste gasoline for nothing, they were to carry a few bombs and deposit them gently, in the course of a large detour, over the Boche lines and cantonments. I was a member of this party. In passing the enemy's lines, we were saluted as usual by the heavy artillery, but we accomplished our mission and came to earth together on the Plateau of Malzeville. The tractors arrived one after another, and every one of them was covered with white dust, which made them look like clowns.

The Plateau of Malzeville is really a part of the dominating heights of Nancy and of the great natural defences of the place, against which the Attila of 1914 threw his hordes. It seems that he was there at the moment of the first attack—in gala costume on horseback, and covered with his big white cloak—ready to make a triumphant entry into the city. He was compelled, how-ever, to turn back stunned and white with impotent rage. That defeat must have cost him dear, for he never repeated the at-tack.

It was one of the great victories of General de Castelnau, for apparently Nancy was not to be defended; General de Castelnau thought differently, however, and he demonstrated the necessity of it.

The plateau was free of any military organization, and the commandant said we could arrange it to suit ourselves; plans were made, tents erected, and on the following day the camp was at least provisionally installed.

"Ah," said I, "there is Do-Hu coming from the mayor's office with his hands full of lodging billets." Every one received one.

"Now," he said, "everybody for himself. It is night, we are in the war zone, and there are no lights in the city; so get on the best way you can."

I looked a long time for the house of my host, for I had eaten nothing during the day. Finally I lost my way and arrived at a bridge which I tried to cross.

"Halt!" called a sentinel.

I made myself known, but he would not recognize me.

"You haven't the password?" he said.

"No," I replied.

"Well, then, you cannot pass!"

"Will you please call the sergeant of the guard?" I asked.

I then explained to the sergeant and he persuaded me not to go to the city, which was too far off; and besides, he said, it was too late, and everything was closed.

"Oh, Lord, and I am so hungry. What do you suppose that little place over there is?" I asked.

"That is a bakeshop."

"And alongside of it?"

"A grocery store."

"Won't they at least give me something to eat there?"

"Oh, I suppose so," he replied.

Four cents' worth of bread, some cheese, and a hard-boiled egg—all washed down with a bottle of wine—three quarters of which I left to the soldiers of the post. It was all swallowed in a very short time.

"Now," said I, "to look for a room." I showed my billet to the sergeant of the guard.

"Do you know these people?" I asked.

"Yes, very well; they are very nice people, and will be glad to take you in."

"Is it far from here?" I asked.

"No; take that street leading up the hill, and the house you want is the second one after passing the fourth street on your left."

I was worn out with fatigue and covered with dust, but I finally arrived and rang the bell. A young girl about twenty years of age opened the door and received me with a pleasant smile; she took my lodging billet and carried it to her mother.

52

"It is a pity, sir, that you have come so late, for you could have dined with us, and we should have had time to prepare your room."

"My dear madam, believe me, I had no choice of the hour of arrival here."

"Never mind, it will really make no difference; my daughter will have my room tonight, and you can take hers. You are worn out, and perhaps you would rather go to bed at once."

"I would prefer to clean up a little first."

"All right: I will show you your room."

"A perfectly charming little place, and what a difference after the smell of oil, grease, and gasoline of our planes!"

"There you are, sir. Goodnight."

"Thank you. I regret very much coming so late; I hope you will excuse me."

After washing, I went to bed promptly and slept the sleep of the just.

Gay as a lark, I ascended the slope which leads to the Plateau of Malzeville, saddened from time to time as I thought of my absent friend Mouchard. The plateau was two hundred meters above the city of Nancy, which was nicknamed "*La Coquette*" and stretched along the slope of the valley.

The ascent to the plateau was very steep, but picturesque, and was studded with pretty cottages, built in little fruit gardens filled with flowers.

Spring had already begun to have its vivifying effect on this charming scene. Trees and bushes were covered early by a tender and beautiful green leafage, in which one could see buds of white and pink flowers ready to burst.

Nature, the great generatrix, heedless of the sound of guns, followed its own wonderful way. After a tour of inspection at the *escadrille*, I took advantage of an invitation of my friend de la Morlaix, and went with him in an automobile to visit Nancy, where the commandant had already gone at the request of the *General Commandant La Place*, and where we saw them both shortly afterwards.

AVIATION FIELD, PLATEAU OF MALZVILLE, NANCY

"Let us go up on the plateau, where we can talk. Are you staying at Nancy, de la Morlaix?"

"For a little while. Commandant," replied de la Morlaix.

"Good morning, Farré. How are you?"

"Very well, indeed. Commandant."

"Have you seen Nancy, and how do you like it?"

"The people are delightful. One can see they have suffered, and are happy at having escaped German occupation. How they love the soldiers, and above all, the aviators."

"Do you think so?" An amused smile spread over his face. "Have you been to the place Stanislas?"

"Yes, sir, it is a perfect little treasure in architecture."

"You weren't familiar with it?"

"I am sorry to acknowledge it, Commandant."

"All right, let's go up. How far along are you with your paintings?"

My period of incubation was finished and my eye practiced; the time had come for me to begin work. We arrived at his house.

"My dear Farré, I am going to tell you my plans, but don't mention them to a soul. The High Command understands the advantage that can be had from the squadron in this place. Look at the chart; there to the northwest you see the German towns, the great factories, the big terminals of Treves, Metz, Strasbourg, Dieuze, Thionville, Saarbruck, Karlsruhe, Ludwigshafen, Manheim, Tribourg, Dillingen, and even Essen. All these places are in our radius of action. What do you think about it?"

"I think, sir, we shall be well able to hold out up to the time of a complete victory over the enemy—that is, until the end of the war."

"That is my opinion, too."

"All right, sir, your plan inspires me; all important events in the air or on the ground will be put on my canvas."

"But then you will certainly have plenty of work."

"What is your next move, sir?"

"I will tell you about that in a few days; at present it is a dead

55

secret, for it is absolutely necessary that the surprise be complete; walls have ears (*il y a de l'espionage dans l'air*)."

CHAPTER 6

Bombing Raids

Our aviation field was laid out. A battery of artillery composed of two pieces of 75 mm. had to be moved, as it interfered with the landing-site.

A lane of cherry trees divided the plateau into two parts. At one end there was a big deserted farmhouse which belonged to a Boche before the war, and which he used as a centre of observation and spying. This was quickly occupied by our flyers and mechanics. The artillery had sawed off two of the largest cherry trees at a height of about one meter and a half. So as to be able to fire more easily on passing enemy planes, that had recently bombarded Nancy, they placed on each one of these stumps one of their pieces. The effect was beautifully picturesque in the midst of our machines, and in looking at these tree-trunks capped with guns, we thought how glorious it was for the cherry trees to die for the service of the country.

There were no flights, or at least very short ones made in simple reconnaissance, the order being not to use the planes in any other way, for they were to be kept ready for anything that the enemy might start. We all wondered what was going to happen, and a week later the commandant called together the pilots and their observers.

"Gentlemen," he said, "we have a glorious mission to accomplish, and' if the weather remains the same tomorrow, the squadron is going to bombard Ludwigshafen. Everybody look at the map."

BOMBARDMENT OF KAHLSRUH BY THE
FIRST BOMBARDMENT GROUP

"That is pretty far off," someone said.

"Look here," said the commandant, who had heard the remark, "what do you mean? I worked it all out and am satisfied that if the weather continues as it is now, we shall have after our return at least fifty quarts of gasoline in our tanks, and besides, these last four days I had you change the tanks with this end in view. Furthermore, Ludwigshafen contains the most important chemical factory in Germany. To be sure, it is a perilous mission, but bear in mind that one well-placed shell will deprive the enemy for some time of one of the most necessary materials in powder-making; the game is worth trying, anyway, and I have full confidence in all of you, and that you will all return."

Proud chief, he never thought of himself.

"All right, gentlemen, and not a word. Study your maps, and tonight you shall have my final instructions. You remain here, Farré; I will not take you tomorrow. Someone has got to stay here as dispatcher," he said to me; but seeing my disappointed look, he added, "There will be plenty of times when you can go, and besides, I promise to give you an exact description of what happens."

It was a beautiful evening, and after dinner, as everyone was present, there was a long discussion between pilots and observers. They studied the maps and the routes which it would be necessary to follow.

"How many shells shall we take along?"

"Well, as for me," said de la Morlaix, "I am going alone. An observer would be bored to death, and besides, I can carry four more shells in his place; that will make at least twelve sugarplums that I shall drop on the heads of those good and dear friends— Ah, the swine! That is all; I am going off to bed. Goodnight, gentlemen, tomorrow at five o'clock."

At this hint everyone got up and went off to rest in preparation for the long raid, the most exhausting and perilous since the opening of hostilities.

At five o'clock the sun rose—an immense globe—the golden glow flooding the plateau with its slanting rays, and revealing the great, patient, inert birds that were waiting the touch of the master hand to inspire them with life and strength. The faithful lark rose with graceful flight into the purple azure, filling the air with his charming and ceaseless warbling, and looking down upon his big brothers, he seemed to call them after him and to be their guide.

The pilots and observers arrived one at a time, and soon were all assembled. Twenty-three planes of each squadron were lined up with their noses to the wind. The weather was the same as the evening before—no perceptible change. The commandant mustered his heroes for their last instructions.

"Well, gentlemen, I trust you understand everything; keep your group intact and follow me; I will lead."

The motors hummed. "They're gassing well," said the machinists.

The commandant took the air, piloted by that skilful pilot, Bunau Varilla; the others followed him at minute intervals, and twenty-five minutes afterward, they were flying above my head, filling the air with a deafening noise, and presenting a wonderful spectacle. They seemed like a swarm of big bees flying through space. They remained ten minutes above the plateau, taking height, and becoming smaller and smaller, until finally like a flight of swans I saw them disappear over Nancy—which was still asleep—and steer to the eastward.

All was now serene on the plateau, except the hearts of men. The larks had once more taken possession of their domain, and sang the return of the winged warriors. Lounging in a chair, I wondered how many of these I should never see again, how many would remain with the enemy, and how many would return.

The contractor for aeroplanes, Voisin, had desired to be present on this occasion.

"I count on a loss of three or four," he said to me, "but no more." There passed two hours of terrible waiting.

Imagining every kind of danger I waited—when at last, I saw on the horizon a black dot—then two, then three, then four.

"There, they are returning!" cried everybody.

The first comer grew larger as he approached; the others followed him closely.

"Was it a good run?" we asked.

"Yes, not bad, but I don't want any more of it."

"You were not prevented from doing your work?"

"No; the surprise was complete; a few cannon shots from the city, but very badly aimed."

"Did you do any damage?"

"Sure. I can say for certain there were at least three or four fires—one of our planes remains—I don't know which one—it was ahead of us. After I had bombarded, I saw him land; his motor must have stopped, for he came down about fifty kilometres from the city."

"Couldn't you make out his plane?"

"No; it was too far off."

"Who could it be?" I thought, distressed beyond measure by doubt and uncertainty.

One after another they came in. We counted ourselves and called to one another—the commandant was absent. It was he, then, and Bunau Varilla who were prisoners. The group was horrified; this loss was the greatest we could have suffered. Our unit had lost its chief, aviation one of its best pilots, and the army one of its finest officers.

It took us a long time to recover from the loss of our chief. De Goys was an accomplished soldier, of fine character, young—about thirty-four—and a true aristocrat; to his high natural qualities he joined a certain amiability that softened his apparent haughtiness. He was a man of simple manners and retiring disposition. All of his subordinates regarded him as a chief of great personal gifts—*sans peur et sans reproche*—who set a high example on every occasion.

He did not remain, however, a prisoner to the end; the French recaptured him, but unfortunately his absence lasted for three years, which were three years of great loss to his country. We met again before my departure on my mission to the United States, and we talked for a long time of his experiences, and he told me how he was forced down.

"Do you remember," he said, "the great care that Bunau Varilla gave to our machine? One never would have thought that our machine would stall. We landed in a field where I hoped at first to make repairs and get away, but I soon found it impossible, as the magneto was done for, so we had to accept the inevitable.

"Bunau looked at me with tears in his eyes. 'We've tried everything, old man, there is no hope.' I told Varilla to set fire to the machine and come and sit with me by the side of the road; they would soon come and take us. Poor old machine—unconscious cause of our lot! We watched it burn with aching hearts. That was its fate; and if it could have talked it would have preferred death rather than serve the enemy. But, old man, the worst of it was to see the rest of our squadron pass over our heads returning to the nest after having accomplished their mission. Seated as we were, side by side, sunk in thought, we groaned over our shattered career. Goodbye to the dreams of heroic exploits; we must now suffer our captivity. Already people were running from all points of the compass; we gave ourselves up; we were prisoners."

"And what about your escape?" I asked.

"We made two attempts; one resulted in my being put in solitary confinement; the second succeeded, however, and here I am."

"But you haven't changed at all and you're looking splendidly."

"Well, I have been three weeks getting back to my old self. I wish you could have seen me before that."

His escape was the result of unheard-of audacity.

But I must get back to my story of the first group. The morale of its personnel was too strong to be affected for any length of time. Captain Wuillermoz, the senior now, took command and organized the first bombardment of Karlsruhe (Duchy of Baden), a more important place than Ludwigshafen; for Karlsruhe was a very smart summer resort, much frequented by the best German society. The raid was determined upon in reprisal for a German raid on Lunéville, which was an open and unfortified town, and where a number of women and children were killed.

From late reports we learned that great importance was attached to this raid. It may be recalled, in passing, that the Queen of Sweden, who was summering at Karlsruhe, lost her head and ran down the street in her nightgown.

Every day some important German factories received a visit from our planes. The Plateau of Malzeville became the most important centre of aviation in the whole army. The first group had just got a new commander; two other groups in the same category had come to join us; they had just been created and made the second and third group, so actually there were nearly a hundred Voisin bombarding planes on the plateau.

Roads were laid out, big hangars at last sheltered the planes, wooden barracks took the place of our tents, which were no longer serviceable; in a word, it was absolute luxury. Aviation felt at last the effects of the public will, and became at once a real air force, gathering under its protecting wings its great mother, the French army.

In June, 1915, there occurred a series of big bombardments. The first group no longer went out alone; the second and third also took part in these, but the first always led, and surpassed, in results, the other two put together. Its new chief possessed in large part the same qualities as de Goys, but he had a different manner of expression. Lieutenant de Vaisseau Cayla was a well-educated young naval officer of good manners; while distinguished-looking, he was of only medium height, and, like all good sailor officers, a fine mess-mate. Beneath his amiability he hid a will of iron and an intrepid courage, amounting at times to recklessness. He soon restored the morale of the group and carefully nurtured it.

The three aviation groups which occupied the plateau at this time were joined by two squadrons of fighting planes of the

BOMBARDMENT OF DILLINGEN BY THE
FIRST BOMBARDMENT GROUP

Nieuport type, all under the command of Commandant Roisin, *dead on the field of honour*. Under his command the bombardments of Dieuze, Metz, Saarbruck, Treves, Dillingen, and Pechelbrunn took place, and other places of military importance as well as important railway stations.

The bombardment of Dillingen was on a larger scale than any yet undertaken; more than sixty planes took part in it. Dillingen was a great industrial centre filled with factories, and its attack caused a great panic among the workers, which lasted for some time. Thanks to that raid, several prisoners who had been forced to work there got away and crossed into our lines, and from them we had an exact account of the result secured by our exploit.

Saarbruck came next, and it cost us dear enough in loss of pilots; Captain Bousquet died there, and his mechanic observer. Bousquet was a fine soldier whom I had known before the war and to whom I became much attached.

The sky was cloudy and it was thought best to attack by taking every advantage of the rifts in the clouds. Just before we began, Captain Bousquet passed on; a shell struck his plane fairly in the middle—so we thought, at least, for we could see a big puff of black smoke spread out over the white cloud, which must have been the bursting of the supply of bombs he carried. Nothing was ever found of them or their machine.

The observer, de Losques, was a brilliant Parisian artist who met death there likewise—both he and his pilot—in a fight with a hostile plane. They crashed to earth within the enemy lines, and military honours were paid them for their brave fight.

I was on the field waiting for the return of my group, which had not yet come in; two were missing—two brothers, Captains Féquant. Albert Féquant, one of the senior French pilots, had made the flight as observer and was piloted by Sergeant Niox; the younger brother, who later took command of one of the most important pursuit groups, was his own pilot, but carried his mechanic as machine-gunner. At that moment he was returning, and I recognized him by the blue star painted on his machine, which was the distinctive sign of the famous V.B. 101 that he commanded. I went up to him.

"How do you do. Captain?"

"Is that you, Farré? I didn't know you with that helmet."

"Was everything O.K.?" I asked.

"Sure," he answered, "but it was tough work. Those damned clouds held us up. Why the devil did we all disperse? There must have been some smash-up. I caught sight of several fights going on; there was one plane in particular that I thought belonged to us, and which I saw I should have to rescue from a bad mess.

"As I made a turn I caught sight of him fighting two Boche Rumplers. I made a half-turn to get to his assistance, a cloud hid them for an instant, and before I could get up with them, out of that cloud came a Boche plane directly for me. Poor thing! He certainly got it in the neck—machine-gun bullets to the left of him and to the right of him, and down he went in flames. There was not the slightest trace of our plane; I suppose he got away—have they all got back?"

"No, Captain, your brother is still missing."

"Oh, he'll get back shortly," said the captain; and peeling off his flying-rig, he passed quietly into his tent.

"What's going on over there?" I said to myself, seeing a gathering crowd of men running towards a plane. As quickly as I could, but with an uneasy presentiment, I joined them and forced my way through the crowd of mechanics. There I found Pilot Niox standing beside his machine, which was painted white, and covered with blood. The body of Albert Féquant hung limply over the edge of the plane. The doctor was there.

"Be careful," the doctor said; "perhaps he is only badly wounded. Bring a stretcher quickly and lift him out gently."

"Has his brother got back ?" asked de la Morlaix.

"Yes," I replied, "go in and see him and break the news to him quietly."

They carried the body into a tent and the nurse stripped it and washed the wounds; there were two balls in the head and one in the arm; the brains were oozing from the skull. "He died instantly," said the doctor, "and did not suffer."

There was no fault to find with the pilot, for from the moment he saw the body of Captain Féquant fall, he retained his presence of mind; he seized the body by the clothing and kept it from falling, and he held it so, flying through space until he landed—a tragic enough landing and the most wonderful in the history of war, past and present. Niox was given the military cross at once and by telephone, as the only just reward for such courage. Captain Féquant's brother, who was told of the loss, did not shed a tear; he bore the shock like a true soldier. His one consolation was the knowledge that he had revenged him without knowing it, and that the man he had brought down was really his brother's slayer.

Such was the life and duty of the bombarding flyers then, and it continues just the same today with only such changes as were made necessary by the constantly improving defence of the enemy.

The heavens are barred up to a certain altitude, which varies in the neighbourhood of four thousand meters; one must pass over enemy lines at least that high, for otherwise one runs the risk of being struck by enemy shells. Even at that altitude it is hard—in fact almost impossible—to get back again without an encounter, for the enemy has been warned and has had time to prepare.

After several of these undesirable experiences, we admitted that night bombardment was an absolute necessity, and to the 101st Squadron, V.B., fell the honour of putting it into practice. This honour was their due, for had not Lieutenant Mouchard and Sergeant Maillard lost their lives at this work six months before?

The railroad station of Metz was our first objective. Captain Laurens, the successor of Captain Féquant, as the latter had been called to command a pursuit group, took charge of the V.B. 101. They bombarded more often at night than they did during the day. The valley of the Meuse and of the Moselle offered splendid objectives; the French factories, manned by the enemy, turned

Tragic return of Captain Albert Féquant

out iron and shells used against us, and it was very necessary to destroy them, to put them out of business. Cantonments, too, made excellent targets, as well as big railroad stations and running trains. The Germans were greatly surprised at these night bombardments, and for a long time were at a loss to know how to defend themselves against an invisible enemy who struck in the dark.

In repelling the attack on Verdun, a steadfast and strong defence was required. The flying squadrons of Malzeville were detached and flew to the rescue of the menaced city. A part of the V.B. 101, which arrived first, took counsel of its previous experience, and harassed the enemy continuously all night. They kept him from getting any rest by dropping bombs on woods, where bivouac fires plainly indicated the position of the troops. On railway stations and on cantonments there was a perfect rain of bombs.

During the daylight hours our fighting planes kept up a series of real aerial battles in which Navarre distinguished himself, and in which Boilot and many others found a hero's death. About a week after this, the supremacy so valiantly striven for fell into our hands, and we remained masters of the air.

As we had so much more to do here than elsewhere, some reinforcements were found necessary, and the second part of Squadron, V.B. 101 and 114 was installed nearby at Autrecourt.

Dear old Mouchard could not be there, but if his body had gone, his spirit remained behind, so that inspired by his memory, our squadron accomplished every night the feats that he had dreamed of, and the Boches made no reply, for they had not yet dared to risk themselves in the dark, though by now we found that very agreeable.

It was about this time that I took part in my first night bombardment, for I had to do and see everything if I was to be a painter of aviation. I rarely mention my paintings, for it does not seem necessary, and I only show them to you as illustrating this book and as an accompaniment as we go along, but they were never made for that purpose.

Chapter 7

Night Bombarding—Autrecourt, Near Verdun—Spring, 1916

A battery truck, loaded, furnishes the light for six powerful searchlights, which amply light the field, and a plane passes in front of them, runs along the lighted surface, soars up from the ground, and disappears in the darkness. The plane is furnished with small reflectors at the side, which are used to make signals in the event of being forced by the stalling of the engine to land in some field; at the end of one wing is fixed a green light, and at the end of the opposite wing a red light. Sailors know what they are—they are "Navigation" lights.

Autrecourt was a little bit of a town of about three hundred inhabitants, and upon our arrival we found it occupied by a half-regiment of artillery; of course, all space was taken. An observation squadron had its cantonment there, and our first visit was to them, for we had not had anything to eat that evening. We accepted with pleasure a part of their supper.

Before long I was elected mess caterer, and in that capacity I was obliged to supply food for all the officers. The village was very poor and had been ransacked, and could only furnish me with some bread. For all other provisions I had to go every morning in an automobile to Bar le Duc, a town about forty kilometres distant, well known for its jellies and jams.

It was the centre of supply for the whole Verdun sector, and all day long the city swarmed with soldiers of every arm, for

General Pétain had established his headquarters there.

Fresh merchandise and provisions of all kinds were snapped up in the twinkling of an eye, and anyone who came to market late went away empty-handed. It was not a very desirable condition in which to return to camp and to one's comrades, for they had chronically empty stomachs, and in order to avoid that situation I always kept on hand a reserve stock of canned goods, which served to meet the necessity.

"Isn't that right Captain?"

"Surely, old man, and then, *à la guerre comme à la guerre.*"

In one of the old houses here, I ran across a good old woman who, for a *franc* a day, was perfectly willing to use her dining-room for the mess, but she added that she expected me to board her besides.

"Of course, my good woman," I said to her. "One person more or less makes no difference."

We were now sleeping in tents; the winter this year was cold and very wet, and it was seldom, indeed, on turning out in the morning, that I failed to step into water. We often longed for the castle of Nancy; at this place there was nothing, a condition which belonged to the beginning of the war. The planes had the same sort of treatment, and were parked in the open. But at last, with the new moon, the weather changed and became fair.

"Say, Farré, we must dine early this evening. If the weather forecast is all right, we will start our first expedition tonight."

"Will you take me Captain?" I ventured.

"No," said he, with a slight hesitation; "I do not know the country well enough yet, and I fear I shall get lost."

"Well, how about tomorrow?"

"If we get along all right today, you shall go."

"All right, sir; and in order to help things along, I have directed the chief cook to roast a half-dozen pheasants, and I have a bottle of Burgundy which I just found."

"That sounds good," he said, his mouth watering; "where did you find all that?"

"We simply went out hunting in an automobile this morning

Night bombardment of the Gare des Sablons, Metz

with Lieutenant Sordet. You can rest assured that it won't be the last one you will eat." And in fact, he regaled himself with them more than once.

"Farré, those pheasants were delicious; we have got to do that over again," said the captain, smoking a ten-cent cigar. "What is the weather outlook for this evening?"

Here is the message. The force of the wind is

5 miles an hour at	5 meters of altitude.
10 miles at	100 meters
5 miles at	300 meters
15 miles at	1000 meters
8 miles at	1200 meters
5 miles at	1500 meters

Looking at it, the captain read out in a loud voice, "Light clouds and fine weather in the early part of the night. That's fine," he said. "We shall start tonight.—Hey, there, Dominic"— the faithful chauffeur of the V.B. 101.

"Sir," replied Dominic.

"Run over to the aviation field and tell them to start the fires. We shall leave in half an hour."

The distance from the aviation field to the village was not more than fifteen hundred yards, which we easily walked.

"All observers and pilots will gather in my tent in flying rig," said Captain Laurens.

There was a bed there, his desk, and a big chart of the Verdun front. Ten minutes later the twenty-four pilots and the bombarding observers were gathered in the tent. This was a solemn moment to the chief, who felt the weight of his responsibility.

"Now, gentlemen, quiet if you please; stop joking, and listen; those who may not understand must say so," he said in a grave voice; and pointing to the chart, he issued his orders and recommendations.

"Partridge will leave first, and the next one will follow five minutes later, and so on throughout, each one's departure being spaced five minutes from the one preceding. You will take your height with lighted navigation lights, flying always to the right; you will leave finally in the direction of the objective after having reached the height of fifteen hundred meters. The return will be accomplished in such and such a place. Now, go ahead, gentlemen!"

It was a perfectly beautiful night, and in my goatskin coat I strolled out of the tent, and reached a small hill, where I could have a view of the entire aviation field, illuminated as it was by six powerful search-lights.

The planes passed in front of these, and throwing their shadows on the ground, they appeared like enormous insects flying around a lighted street-lamp. The noise of the motors, the flames, and the torches placed about the field made it look like a night fair. The first passed through the lighted zone, headed upwards, and disappeared in the darkness; five minutes later the second, and afterwards the ten others followed. Soon I saw above me only shooting stars moving slowly. The humming of the motors grew less and less, and the camp was left in silence.

Lying flat on the ground, I followed with my eyes the twelve bright spots moving towards the enemy lines; as they approached them, their lights went out and they gave no sign of their passage, except the noise of their motors. The ground was shaking under me; for fully an hour the heavy artillery had been bombarding Verdun. Great lights illuminated the horizon, then went out, and then again lighted the entire heavens; they kept on incessantly—keeping the sky constantly illuminated.

We replied, and I could make out very well the shells of our guns, and could distinguish readily the flights of our projectiles and those of the enemy as they buried themselves in the earth, and bursting with terrific prolonged sounds seemingly tore up the ground. Search-lights swept the heavens for our planes; when one was found, all guns took it for a target. Flare rockets, a German invention, intended to set us on fire, moved through the air. "What a grand and tragic scene, and how beautiful viewed from our planes," I murmured.

"Tomorrow," I said to myself, "I shall be there with them."

This heavy bombardment continued with a deafening noise. I was interrupted in my sad meditations by the faint noise of a motor, slowly getting louder and louder. Its searchlight was looking for the landing, like a railroad train entering a station, asking with its whistle if the road is clear. This was the first to come back, and the others appeared in turn, planing down and gracefully taking ground. In the captain's tent, one by one, they made their reports, which were immediately sent to the Headquarters Staff.

Midnight, and time to go to bed! I lighted a cigarette and turned in, lulled to sleep by the fierce bombardment, which kept up continually.

At daybreak I was awakened by more cannon shots; I arose and put my head out of my tent. The sun shone in the soft sky; the bursting of shells from our anti-aircraft guns placed little tufts of smoke upon the azure of the sky.

"There's a Boche; he's coming back to give us a run for our money."

I hastily dressed myself and ran out to see what had happened.

My comrades were grumbling. "Why is he coming to bother us now? Can't he let us alone? Why doesn't he do as we do and fly at night, the lazy dog!"

He was now over the village; I saw his bombs drop. They struck at one side, raising clouds of dust. One failed to explode but made a dull sound. Now he was directly over us. I threw myself on the ground face down—although I had only one chance in a thousand of being struck. Ah, he was turning around! He had taken fright at another little black point—one of our planes. Unfortunately, however, the Boche was too high; we could not reach him before he had returned within his lines.

It was only six o'clock; what should I do? Not go to bed again, certainly. It was a superb morning, so I took my box of colours and started to work, putting on canvas what I had seen the evening before.

We had now a succession of beautiful nights; the moon rose

late, and we waited until it was high in the heavens before starting on our expedition. The day before, the Captain had given me permission to make my first night flight, but luck was against me. Unaccountably, the machine refused to work; after having left the earth, and entered into complete darkness at an altitude of one hundred meters, I noticed a thumping in the motor; the machine turned her nose downward, being no longer pushed by her own power, and I wondered what we were going to fall on.

Captain Laurens, knowing that he had to land—that it was inevitable—shut off his gas to prevent a fire, if possible. The machine struck the ground with a terrific shock, bounded into the air, and ricocheted several times over a ploughed field, but our little search-light saved us; an enormous tree was right ahead, and the captain had just time to give a quick turn to the steering-wheel, which threw the plane to the right.

"Look out for the bombs!" he said; "they might explode. See if they have moved. Weren't you paralyzed with fear?"

"No; to tell you the truth, I didn't have time to be afraid. The plane is pretty well broken up."

"Oh, it's done for; anyhow, our show is over for this evening."

The machinists, attracted by our searchlight, came running, bringing with them a stretcher.

"Thank you for your kind attention," I said. I had a bad blow on the head, but all the same, I felt the stretcher to be superfluous.

"Look here," said one, "you don't seem to appreciate that you had a narrow escape; it was one out of a hundred."

The Captain was angry at having missed his flight. He was present when his pilots left, resigned enough to his fate, but not happy.

The next night I had my second trial.

"I shall not take you," said the captain; "I want to go much farther than the objective set by the General Headquarters of the army, I will look up an observer who is lighter than you; it

76

is absolutely necessary."

I thought to myself that it was simply a pretence, and that he was superstitious. I didn't stop to argue with him, but inquired if there was a pilot without an observer.

"I am one," said Sergeant Fernand, a man whom I did not know; "my observer is sick, and if you want to take me, we will go together."

"Fine! Let's go to it!"

The target for the night was the railroad station at G. P., about forty kilometres in the rear of the enemy's lines; the signal reports stated that there was great concentration of material and troops at that point; doubtless the enemy was going to take advantage of the darkness to place these to best advantage, and it was necessary to prevent this.

Fernand was a good pilot, and a man who took care of his own plane. I inspected our bombs and then got into the machine; the motor ran beautifully and we started along at good speed. We soon left the ground and commenced our night voyage; I kept my ears on the motor and my eyes in front of me.

It was a beautiful night, with no wind except that made by the speed of the machine. At first, my eyes were blinded by the passing rays of searchlights; I could see absolutely nothing. Little by little, I recovered my normal vision, however, and I could make out the contours of the ground. There was a village just beneath us; the houses apparently in ruins, while a yellow light filtered through some of the windows, resembling fireflies in the grass.

I could make out the roads and a little river which wound around, reflecting in places the silvery light of the moon. We kept turning continually towards the right, all lamps and searchlights going, not only from those beneath us, but from our friends above. I glanced at the ground—it appeared in miniature; I looked at the altitude, and it read one thousand meters. The last of the planes had left the ground and disappeared. We had all started.

The sky was a beautiful bluish-green; the moon brilliant, and

RETURN FROM A NIGHT BOMBARDMENT – LANDING FIELD

the surrounding stars pale in comparison; light clouds, visible in the moonlight, moved slowly with it like an escort.

Before getting into the danger zone, I thought of the motor. It seemed normal—yes, no pounding, and cylinders perfect and not heated. I could now devote myself to contemplation of the scene for the next ten minutes. Every faculty was alert—my thoughts ran riot; eyes and brain worked together. One passed along to the other everything I saw, whether material or immaterial. We shut our navigation lights; we heard the guns firing furiously beneath us—it was like wild fireworks.

Everywhere there were rockets and fuses detonating with all the colours of the rainbow for minutes at a time—then suddenly going out. Some of these were flare rockets. I could clearly see the barrage fire of the 75's falling in our own lines, the big guns joining their thunderings in a common voice, loud and strong. Sometimes a light remained after the bursting of a shell, and in that case we knew that something had caught fire. Farther back I saw an immense light; it was the city of Verdun burning. High in the heavens, and not far above us, great shells were bursting.

Fernand slapped me on the knee, and pointing to a plane, he said, "There's one getting it in the neck; what's he after, anyway?"

"He is now passing over Romagne. There are the three searchlights of the aviation field looking for him. Ah! they have him! No! the idiots have lost him! They could not have seen him!"

The chasers got under way and went up like serpents in the heavens.

"Ah," I said, "look out—there's one of them coming our way."

"Heavens, yes!—but I still have time to dodge him."

A little turn, and I saw it pass within a hundred meters of us. I had a chance to observe that particular engine of war—ten or twelve incendiary globes connected by a chain. I wonder what their motive power is; do they go up by their own action, or are they fired from guns?

Without knowing it, we got into the thick of a fight, and we ran lightly to the sound of the guns. At one time the enemy's searchlights blinded us, but by a sudden twist of the helm, we shot out of the glare, leaving our place vacant for those who followed us. Calm returned to us; we were back of the Boche lines, steering straight for a bright light, which was G. P. In saying that calm re-established itself I should add that, since the start, there had really been no disturbance of it; the noise of the engine was preeminent and prevented any of the other noises reaching us. The result was that we saw everything and heard nothing, except perhaps a belated cannon shot, which burst about fifty meters from us, right in our wake, giving us a forward blast.

"Are we steering in the right direction?" asked Fernand.

"Yes," said I; "it's right over there."

From time to time I looked over my shoulder to verify our position; it would never do to lose sight altogether of the searchlights of our camping-ground. Yes—they were directly behind us; small—oh, so very small! Off to the left were those of Clermont and to the right those of Souilly; so far, so good.

We were approaching our goal—a kilometre more only; but already the enemy had been bombed; he had hastily put out all lights, excepting only those, of course, which our shells had lighted.

I noticed several fires. It was our turn now, and I dropped one—two—three—four bombs; again—one—two—three—four bombs, at intervals, over our goal, and as I bent over, I could see seven explosions, and out of the seven, one caused a new fire.

"But what has become of my eighth bomb?" I wondered.

I pushed my arm into the bomb release and then looked outside, when—horror of horrors—there it was, suspended from a cable underneath our machine.

"My God, Fernand, one of the bombs is hanging by a cable! Have you got a cutter to clear it away?"

"No; but we've got to get rid of it at all costs, for if it explodes, in three seconds we are gone; I don't want to make a landing with that thing hanging there under the plane; in fact, I would prefer to be blown to heaven in little bits from here."

"Well, we shan't go that way," I said.

I struggled with my knife in my efforts to cut the cable; it was of steel, and I could not get through it; but my hand was not of steel, and I cut a deep gash in it. What to do was the question. We could not be thinking of it much longer, and finally, I hauled in the bomb by the cable; it weighed about fifteen kilos. I seized it, raised it above my head as far as possible, and threw it down with all my strength. The cable parted, and the shell was lost in space.

"That's over," said Fernand.

"Yes," said I.

"Never," he sighed, "never again, for hereafter I shall carry a cable-cutter."

I looked over, and saw that between us and the ground the shell had exploded in a beautiful and innocent piece of fireworks.

We had now turned about and were returning towards the border of France, following along the edge of the Argonne Forest. Around Verdun everything was still illuminated and under fire; the bursting of bombs was continuous—big and little interspersed. I was sorry that the noise of the motor prevented me from hearing; on the other hand, I thought that such a touch of materialism would spoil the seemingly unreal beauty of that terrible reality.

Fernand passed me an object which he drew out of the pocket of his teddy bear.

"What is that?" I inquired.

"Taste it."

I touched it to my lips; it was a delicious brand of old Burgundy. Ho!—delightful!—just the thing! It was getting very chilly, and I had suddenly a mad desire to smoke a cigarette. That mouthful of alcohol reminded me of worldly things. We had now recrossed the lines, and the pilot relighted his navigation lights.

NIGHT BOMBARDMENT AND EXPLOSION OF AN ENEMY
AMMUNITION DUMP AT COUCY-LES-EPPES

"Not yet, Fernand," said I; "let's remain up here alone in the heavens."

The moon was now ahead of us, sailing rapidly westward, escorted by a crowd of little plump clouds, silvered over with its shining light. The Argonne Forest stretched along beneath with its deep ravines, in which a light fog could be noticed. Bivouac fires were visible through the heavy atmosphere, and a white smoke like a silver thread suspended from above rose towards us.

Fernand pointed with uplifted arm and I followed his direction. One of our planes, coming between us and the moon and advancing towards us, passed less than twenty meters overhead; we were invisible to him, and I trembled at the thought of the narrow margin of escape from a collision, and cursed the pilot who failed to follow the rules of the road, by returning on the going-out route.

The fires of our camp were now getting very near. The light fog rose up from it, forming, a thousand meters below us, a soft bed of transparent gauze. Little by little it became more dense— now it had the appearance of a calm sea; nevertheless, all our planes were able to get back and land in time, before the fog got so thick as to hide the ground.

Our reports made, everyone came in exhausted. I fell on my bed completely worn out; my brain was filled with everything that I had experienced; my eyes tired, my body bruised. It was four o'clock in the morning, and I heard the lark rising with the sun and taking his morning flight in the first breaking of the dawn. I fell asleep lulled by its sweet, melodious song, happily unconscious of all I had seen and felt.

CHAPTER 8

Partridge

The next day, I had the great pleasure of again meeting Partridge, whom I had not seen for two months. He was a lad about twenty years of age at the beginning of the war. I met him at St. Pol; he was a mechanic in the First Escadrille, V.B. 101, in company with Mouchard.

At Camp Melette he was at the front, and having had considerable experience under fire, he soon became one of the most accomplished pilots. Beardless, impetuous, with a bland expression of countenance, there was nothing about him that indicated the man of war. Calm and quiet, he placidly came and went over the enemy's lines, careless of danger and happy in doing his duty; I never left him. Now he is a lieutenant and in command of the celebrated *escadrille* organized by his own idolized superior, Mouchard; there was no one living more entitled to that honour.

Installed near us at Lemne was the first part of the *escadrille*, the grounds not being large enough to hold us all. He came in a plane on Sunday morning with his observer. Lieutenant de Langlade, to make us a visit.

"Hello, you here. Partridge! Goodmorning, Langlade."

"Goodmorning, sir."

"You will take luncheon with us, of course."

"With pleasure, sir."

"Of course, Farré, there are partridges on the menu, are there not?" the captain asked mischievously.

LIEUTENANT PARTRIDGE

"I think so, Captain. At all events, there are some good wild pigeons and a wild duck."

"Gracious, it'll be a regular wedding breakfast!"

We all started off to the little church of Autrecourt, to attend high mass, and found the church crammed with army men. After our return we talked over times past and present, happy to see each other again.

"How many bombardments have you made since the beginning of the war. Partridge?"

"I think I have just about made my 180th—those that you know, like Ludwigshafen, Karlsruhe, Treves, Dieuze, Pechelbrunn, Saarbruck, Dillingen, and so on."

"And how many hours have you spent flying over the enemy country?"

"More than eight hundred."

"What! Not wounded yet?"

"No wounds, and don't you think it singular!" he said; and, laughing, he added, "I must touch wood, for as late as yesterday, de Langlade and I just missed paying dearly for all we had escaped."

"What do you mean?"

"We were almost smothered by a shell during our night flight."

"How do you mean by a shell?"

"Why—by one of our own shells."

"But I don't understand."

"It's all very simple. We were behind Verdun, and de Langlade insisted upon dropping a bomb upon some Boche searchlights which had given us trouble every time we came over that sector. He held on to his last bomb and was holding it in his arms. How I fainted, I can't understand, but when I came to, we were about five hundred yards above the ground; the unguided plane had descended slowly like a dead leaf.

"Weak as I was, I had just strength enough to get my balance and turn and glance around; I saw de Langlade fallen over in his seat, and still holding his shell, which emitted a very pestilential odour. The liquid it contained had run all over him, burning his clothes. I shook him and struck him a blow in the face, bringing him to at last.

"'Where are we?' he asked.

"'Well, my son, I can't tell you,' I answered.

"'What is this I have hold of here?'

"'Why, it is your shell; it has just failed to send us both to glory. Throw it overboard.'

"'Not yet, please; just show me where the Boches are. If I can hold it, I don't intend to let this last one go for nothing.'

"I looked over the side and watched; we were directly over the searchlights. 'There they are; they are searching for us!' I exclaimed.

"'Ah, the swine!' cried de Langlade; 'a little more and we were gone! More to the right, if you please; head her up to the wind. What height are we now?' he asked.

"'Eight hundred meters,' I replied.

"'Oh, the fools! They are trying to reach us at fifteen hundred meters. I think that I am all right now. There they are.'

"Then, after a moment of silence—'Right over him now, old chap; look out for him!' I leaned over and there wasn't a sign of the searchlights, only pitch-dark night—everything had gone out. We certainly had a narrow escape."

"Well, is that little illness which you had all gone?" I asked.

"Quite gone—fresh air is a wonderful cure."

"Your raid must have been pretty long—at least two hours."

"Yes, all of that—and do you know what we did after we returned to the *escadrille*?"

"I think you probably treated yourself to some preserves and a bottle of Burgundy."

"Yes—but after we had filled our tanks for another raid."

"Partridge, coming from you that doesn't astonish me in the least. You must take me above the clouds one of these days; I want to see them and study them."

"Whenever you wish. Master."

"Ah, my dear boy, not Master."

"Yes, sir, why not?"

"Because a man is never Master in my profession."

Two months later, dear old Partridge in trying out a new plane fell to earth and broke both legs. Fortunately for him, the accident took place at Compiègne, where Dr. Carrell, an American, had his clinic at the time, and thanks to him both legs were restored, although somewhat shorter than before.

CHAPTER 9

Observation Flying

The observation squadron, by which is meant the squadron of planes that reports the fall of shots, was located near us and commanded by Captain d'Aimery. Their work was very different from ours; it began when we finished, and I admit very frankly that their task was less appreciated and was more dangerous. They are the most useful auxiliaries to the army; they report the fall of shots and signal the necessary sight corrections to the guns. Their work is inconspicuous—never seen; they fulfil their mission and fall heroically without any mention in dispatches, victims of the enemy's guns and planes.

One morning—his suspicion of my being a hoodoo gone—I spoke to Captain Laurens of my desire to assist in the work of some of these observation planes.

"That 's all right, my dear man, we are not flying tonight, however,—will tomorrow do?"

"Certainly, sir."

"Ask d'Aimery, then, what time they begin tomorrow, and we can put in the spare time by running over the lines. I want to see the Verdun sector in daylight; flying at night all the time is monotonous. Don't you find it so?"

"Ah, I am delighted to hear you say that. I never dared to ask for the chance to fly during the day."

The next morning at seven o'clock, we flew towards the Vauquois sector, where the guns were in full swing. There were two spotting-planes of the Farman type, in which our best observers were at work at an altitude of about eighteen hundred meters. Keeping as nearly head to wind as possible, they described circles of about a kilometre's radius, noting the point of fall of the shots from our long-range guns. For about a quarter of an hour we made big circles around them, observing them.

The observer, by means of his wireless, advised the artillery and directed their fire up to the time that they hit the mark. When this was reported, the gunners made careful note of the angle of fire and the direction. Such work is always tedious and dangerous, because the enemy never sees with any pleasure an enemy plane taking notes over his head, for he knows perfectly well that these observations may be followed by terrible consequences for him.

To do away with this, the enemy's special airguns, which he uses constantly and often with great effect, try to bring down that human bird which stubbornly remains up there as long as our guns continue to fire. Sometimes when the shrapnel shells come very close, the observation planes rise three or four hundred meters to avoid being hit.

Another danger to the observation plane is attack from fighting planes; swift, handy, and heavily armed, like hawks they dart from the upper heights down upon their inoffensive prey. This comparison is particularly apt in the case of the Farman plane, which is called a chicken coop because it resembles a chicken coop in shape. The Farman is an excellent planer, too. Head to the wind, he can be held so that he doesn't appear to move; swift, and as well-balanced as a butterfly, he toys with the wind and can maintain his position with ease.

He has no speed; his defence is limited; that is to say, he is without protection from the enemy who attacks him from behind, so that if the fighting planes do not protect him, he is lost from the start. No gallantry will save him—we are not living in the Middle Ages. The swifter enemy, taking advantage of his own speed, will take position in rear of his prey, where he is unprotected, and shoot the poor dove down.

Unfortunately, in order to protect the efficiency of these precious birds, a great number of scouting planes are required, and we have not got them. I should add that this regulation requiring a plane to remain steady, scarcely pleases our flyers; they much prefer joy-riding around. This is the mission of the observation planes, which is often combined with aerial photography.

"There you are, Farré; have you observed long enough?"

"Yes, sir," I replied. And we left the two planes to continue their circles, nursed by the wind and with the noise of the motor accompanied by shrapnel of every calibre.

An immense cloud of smoke, covering the ground over a great extent, hid half a city; it was Verdun. I made out distinctly the cathedral, near which we lived. The fortress alongside of it was still unattacked, or appeared so, at least. "Poor old city, what you have suffered, and how much you will still suffer," I thought; "your martyrdom is not over yet."

The Captain pointed with his hand. "Douaumont," he said, indicating it in the distance, "and Dead Man's Hill, the Fort of Vaux, and Hill number 304; all are gone."

The woods were razed, the ground torn up, and the houses in ruins. The country appeared to be uninhabited; it looked like a continent of the moon; nothing was visible; nothing moved. The most frightful cataclysm could not have devastated the country more. Notwithstanding that, thousands of men were there like worms and microbes in a dead body, working to consume themselves.

The big guns were very active; heavy shells threw up columns of earth and smoke in answer; they seemed the only living things. In the rear of our lines—for here the trenches no longer existed, being replaced by shell-holes which touched each other in a continuous line—I noticed beautifully constructed trenches entirely new, made by our engineers. The sight of them was a great comfort to me: Verdun was not yet taken, because a new barrier to France was placed there, more insurmountable than all the others.

I was interrupted in my reflections by the sight of a fighting plane hovering around our position. He afforded us the pleasing

MOTOR CAUDRON SIGNALLING THE POSITION OF INFANTRY AND
TAKING PHOTOGRAPHS, SOMME, 1916

spectacle for five minutes of manoeuvring in the air with side-slopes, dives, looping-the-loop, going and coming around us like a fly following a moving animal.

"That is Navarre in his red Nieuport!" I called to the captain.

"Well, I'll tell you what, old chap, if that was a Boche, we should have long since been finished."

All at once he disappeared. The captain, turning to the right and left, made every effort to find him again, but without result. He succeeded in holding himself in such a position that we could not make him out, and played hide-and-seek with us; it would have been easy, indeed, for him to approach and destroy us. We were in this situation for about five minutes, and had been moving towards the enemy's lines; their guns paid no attention to us. Nevertheless, I felt we were in the danger zone.

"Shall I get the machine gun ready captain?"

"It would be a good idea. We are sure to fall in with a Boche plane sooner or later, as we are almost in their country."

In fact, just then one appeared, and he was coming down directly upon us.

"That's a big biplane—a Rumpler," said the captain; "hit him."

We steered straight for him, but he passed us about two hundred yards to the right.

"Ta, ta, ta, ta," spoke the machine gun as we opened up on him. He responded as quickly, and then disappeared; each of us immediately made a half-turn with the intention of coming up with each other again.

But what should I suddenly see, high in the air above us like a meteor—Navarre, in his red plane, driving through the mist, a veritable bird of prey, swooping down upon the poor Rumpler, almost touching it with his wings. A volley from his machine gun set fire to its gasoline tank, and it dived down through the space that separated us from the ground.

One would, indeed, have a heart of stone if one were not moved by that tragic sight. Quick as lightning, the plane fell

VICTORY OF NAVARRE, VERDUN, 1916

disabled, trailing behind it an enormous tail of smoke from the burning gasoline in the tank. Is it possible that the occupants remained unscathed? Imagine, if you can, the torture of those two human beings during the five minutes they spent before they crashed to earth. I pray God they had a swift death. The conqueror swept in a spiral of glory around that colossal torch as it descended from the heavens, an easy victory for him.

"That is the fate reserved for those who fly in other than fighting planes."

"Yes," said the captain, "that's so. Now let's go and see Navarre."

We soon reached Vadelincourt repair station and came to earth; Navarre had arrived there only a moment before, and was stretched out under the wing of his plane. The terrible fighter apparently was not thinking of his recent victims.

"Well, you certainly did come from heaven. Where were you at the time?" I said.

"Well, this is how it was. I was sure that you were going to be attacked, and so I kept on flying two thousand yards above you. When I saw the Boche, I headed straight for him and let fly a full belt in my machine gun."

"Then you made use of us as bait," said the captain.

"Absolutely," he said.

"Do you think you killed the pilots?" said I, the thought of their terrible death holding me.

"Oh, yes, they must have been struck fifty times. They probably never suffered a thing. You may have seen that the plane had lost control when it fell."

"So much the better," I said.

Upon our return, we fell in with a bi-motor Caudron whose observer had been photographing enemy positions.

CHAPTER 10

Aerial Photography

Aviators having charge of this kind of work—which consists in photographing the ground occupied by the enemy—have very much the same sort of duty as that of the observation planes. Their duty is usually performed in the bi-motor Caudron. Often these men accomplish the two missions of observing and photographing at the same time.

Such a double service was not anticipated by the General Staff before the war began, but neither was trench warfare; it is evident that trench warfare made all that necessary, according to the old French proverb, *The need creates the means*, and all these different kinds of service were organized on the front under the fire of the enemy.

I cannot say who originated it; several captured planes were found to carry photographic apparatus, and were particularly adapted to this special kind of work. In our own army, this particular service was highly perfected and very well organized. Every army corps had its own squadron, used especially for photographing enemy positions, and therefore each army corps doing this work made it possible to have snapshots of the whole front from Dunkerque to Belfort. These photographs were almost always taken vertically and at about the same altitude, and afterwards joined together, thus forming a complete map in which every detail stands out clearly. Shell-holes can be seen with the naked eye.

The reader will, no doubt, understand the reason of the new

branch of service called camouflage, which, by the use of false trees, or tents painted the same colour as the ground, renders things almost invisible; in fact, this is the only means known for hiding from the eye of the aviator, or from the exposures made by the lenses of his camera, important works and emplacements of guns; unfortunately, it is not possible to camouflage everything.

Imagine, if you can, the enormous amount of this kind of work which is accomplished; and that is not all, it is necessary to keep it up to date, and that is what gives real interest to it. For example, the Staff receives from the aviators a series of photographs of a certain sector; a few days later it suspects that the enemy has made important changes, and at once orders new series of pictures; if only one single tree is added, it is immediately detected, and our own dispositions are regulated accordingly.

Just before an attack such operations are carried out along the entire front and are made as complete as possible. Before commencing a bombardment of the enemy's defences, the batteries have in their hands charts as carefully made as possible from photographs of these defences, and they make use of them in the bombardment. During such an attack the observation planes see if the fire is effective and well directed, and when it is finished the plane skims along at a low height over the trenches to see if all the enemy defences are destroyed, such as barbed wire, telegraph lines, machine-gun nests, etc., and if a man shows himself the flyer takes advantage of it. At such times the soldiers are most certainly to be found in their dugouts, where they are often engulfed and buried alive; in that way many have been killed.

This work is of the most dangerous kind for the planes engaged in it. They are obliged to fly at a very low height—not more than three hundred meters—right through the danger zone; and when it rains, or clouds are hanging very low, they come down to not more than one hundred meters above the ground, and at this low altitude they very often become the victims of bursting shrapnel. All honour to those unknown he-

FARMAN BIPLANE OBSERVING THE DESTRUCTION BY THE FIRE OF
THE ALLIED ARTILLERY OF THE ENEMY TRENCHES AND OTHER
DEFENCES AT THE MORT HOMME, VERDUN, 1916

roes who do this important duty so bravely, without thought of special glory or honour!

Here is a tragic history of a Boche plane which was engaged in observing and spotting work; it was in Champagne that this thrilling drama took place, and it demonstrates the French bravery and spirit carried to the extreme, where all consciousness of danger is lost in the performance of straight duty.

Every night at the same hour, an enemy aviator came to take photographs and to make observations over our lines in Champagne. He appeared to be invulnerable, and apparently without any regard for danger he came regularly and accomplished his mission. Our artillery was powerless to bring him down from his celestial height, and our pursuit planes always arrived too late. Two of our planes had been brought down by him, and it was to avenge our two comrades and to pay the enemy for his audacity that we now prepared.

The pilots of a scouting escadrille of the Nieuport type were camped near us, and were wild with rage at their inability to catch him. Three of them, however, swore to do so, and among them was the Quartermaster de Terline, who solemnly swore to get him. "If my shot won't do it," he said, "I will run him down and fall with him."

Half an hour before the usual time of his arrival, there was de Terline cruising at two thousand meters, which was about the height at which the Boche habitually flew. De Terline noticed that he was the one farthest off from the Boche; and he saw his two comrades attacked and one after another withdraw from the fight, and nose-dive down to their landing-field, compelled to do so by their machine guns getting jammed.

But de Terline did not know this, and supposed his two comrades were killed, and so it was with a rage amounting almost to fury that he increased his speed to get above the Boche. When in a proper position he dropped, and rammed his terrible enemy. The collision brought them together inextricably, so that, spinning around in the air, we saw them fall tragically to the ground from about one thousand meters, and crash to earth in a mass of formless debris.

In this way French aviators carry out their promises; and never again did an enemy come every day at the same time to accomplish his mission over the lines of Champagne.

During all these observations my leisure time was given up to painting. I would have liked very much to work on one subject for a long time, but, unfortunately, that was impossible. I had to follow the events and could not give my canvases all the time and work which their importance deserved. I tried my best to preserve a truly historical picture in an artistic way, and certain paintings show a deep study of the subject. I do not say that they are any the better for that, though several have obliged me to return a number of times and fly over the ground again, in order to correct inaccuracies. Vauquoi was one of these. I determined to portray in that one the exact topography of the ground, destroyed villages, shell-holes, and the trenches. As soon as they were finished, I sent them to the Army Museum, where they were exhibited among those by comrades in the *Salon d'Honneur.*

I received a friendly letter from Lieutenant de Vaisseau de Laborde, who belonged to the first bombardment group commanding the centre of the maritime aviation at Dunkerque, in which he said there was something besides land aviation in this war, and he invited me to pass a few days with him, telling me I would get into a real war atmosphere; that the history of aviation in connection with Dunkerque was already rich in exploits, and if I would like to go with them and bombard Zeebrugge, I had only to say the word.

"Well, this is going to alter my arrangements somewhat," I said, "but put in my request to go."

The quartermaster understood the situation, and a fortnight later I presented myself before the admiral commanding at Dunkerque, who gave me a cordial welcome.

CHAPTER 11

At Dunkerque, March, 1916

De Laborde introduced me to all his officers (all naval officers, of course), and I was quartered in a fine, large, and well-lighted room.

"Will you be all right here, and Can you work?" asked de Laborde.

"Perfectly," I answered.

The population of Dunkerque was about equal to that of Nancy; the people were sympathetic and kind. Several buildings—notably the cathedral, of which the roof had been blown off—carried marks of the numerous 480 mm. shells fired from the long-distance guns of the Germans.

Alongside of our centre of maritime aviation there was installed a British aviation group, a squadron of scouting Sopvitch hydroplanes, and bombarding hydroplanes of the Shor type. Their operations were made separately, but with the same end in view, that of fighting the enemy hydroplanes and their submarines, for which both Ostend and Zeebrugge were repair bases.

At Dunkerque there was a little bay which formed the anchorage, but it was entirely too small for our hydroplanes to take the air. They were obliged to thread their way out and in like seagulls, and pass between the masts of the boats, so that often a wing touched, and then—up! a rapid half-turn and bang!—down into the water, from which they were very often fished out in a sad condition. One would not believe it, but a fall into the sea is really more sudden and hard than a fall to the earth.

Lieutenant de Laborde was a fine leader; he understood aviation from the bottom up, had been a pilot before the war, and had broken a leg at it. It was on account of his known worth in this branch that the Minister of Marine selected him to organize this centre of maritime aviation. I was astonished at the completeness of the installation; in the centre was a very fine pigeon cote, where a special detail had been made to take entire charge of the three hundred birds which made this their home.

The pigeon mail was a distinctly valuable auxiliary, truly useful, even indispensable. Whenever a plane went out on an expedition, four birds were taken along in a little cage, and in case of the engine stopping, or of damage, or of a forced descent to the water after a flight, the pigeons were freed, and carried back to the home base the S.O.S. calls of the aviators.

Before beginning to paint the exploits of the pilots, I wished to see this new machine with which I was not familiar, and de Laborde opened for me the four big hangars which sheltered fifteen planes.

"Aren't they beautiful?" he asked.

"Yes, they certainly are," I answered; "but what do those three letters, F. B. A., indicate?"

"France, Beige, Anglo," he replied, laughing.

"I don't believe you—really?"

"No—they are really the initials of the firm that makes them."

They were certainly beautiful in shape, with splendid lines, and when I saw them fly for the first time, they seemed like gigantic fish leaving the ocean for the realms of the sky.

I immediately got to work; I drew and painted them from every aspect, and in every position on the ground, in the air, and on the water, and after making about a dozen studies I was reasonably familiar with their appearance; then I decided to begin something big, but first I thought it was necessary to make a flight in one of them.

The commandant was very much pleased with these studies, and I asked him when he would fly.

102

EXPLOIT OF CAPTAIN BONE, THE ENGLISH AVIATOR,
OVER THE NORTH SEA, 1915

"Ah, my dear sir, I am distressed beyond words; I go on no more expeditions. I just got a letter from the Admiralty prohibiting the commanding officer from taking part in any flights, but I can give you la Burthe—he is an excellent pilot."

"Oh, it doesn't make any difference, Commandant," I said.

"I believe tomorrow they will undertake a flight to Zeebrugge. Would you like to go?"

"I certainly would, sir."

CHAPTER 12

Bombarding of Zeebrugge

Time, nine o'clock in the morning; weather, a little thick, trying to clear; sun shining through the light covering of clouds; the air fresh; truly it had every prospect of being a fine day.

The orders were that no expedition should start with fewer than four planes. It was necessary to be able to meet the attacks of the Boche squadrons, which went out always in great numbers.

"My, isn't our little birdie beautiful," said la Burthe; "and what a bully engine; it must be at least one hundred horse-power."

It hummed wonderfully; it was an Ispano Suiza.

"Look here, la Burthe, I don't want to bombard. I would prefer to remain in the rear as a spectator, in order to see better, if we can do that."

"Oh, all right, then, we will leave our bombs behind."

"My word, no; perhaps we shall run across a submarine; it is a rare species, but the chance is so fine!"

Everyone else had gone on.

"Come on," said la Burthe.

"I'm all ready."

"And your life preserver?"

"I've got it."

"Good!" The motor was started up at full speed.

"But the pigeons—my God! quick, bring them," said la Burthe to the mechanic.

I grabbed up these precious birds jumbled close together in

the cage.

The hydroplane was drawn to its starting-place and then turned around and started. We opened the throttle, and the water flew up on each side in a silver fringe. As the speed increased, the engine tried to clear the water; finally it lifted entirely and moved forward, striking the crests of the waves only in little short blows. Very soon this stopped and the machine left the water entirely, and rose majestically into the air, with its pilot steering skilfully between the ships' masts until we finally emerged from amongst them. Dunkerque was spread under us; we were at sea—the three other planes were already far away.

Zeebrugge was about forty kilometres distant as the crow flies, and with a fair wind a half-hour was enough to allow for this flight; and always the same question of a pilot to a new passenger.

"How goes it .? All right .?" he asked me.

"Splendid," said I.

We were already near the end of the route; the three others made a detour to allow us to catch up to them.

"We will steer offshore to avoid the coast batteries," said the pilot to me, "and go straight on to Zeebrugge. We are now about fifteen miles from the mole. Ah, the famous mole! I can see it well, protecting the port formed by the canal."

"There are the Boche submarines," cried la Burthe, "and the hydroplanes are on the mole. Can you make out their hangars there, with the roofs shining? We are discovered; the heavy coast guns are amusing themselves by firing at us. See those big bursts; they are at least 210's; a shell that size must cost something!"

"But they don't fire with them only?"

"Oh, no, you will see the 77's when you are closer. We are going to remain in the rear."

"Yes, if you don't mind. Can you hold her about five hundred yards from the others?"

"That is more dangerous, for we may be struck by some wild shots," said la Burthe, laughing.

There was little shipping in the harbour, only a few destroyers within the break-water.

"No submarines?" I asked.

"Oh, don't worry," said la Burthe; "they don't wait until we are on top of them before they plunge. Ah, there are the Boche hydroplanes getting under way. Bernie, old chap, you will get there too late."

Our three planes had arrived and their six bombs fell just in front of the canal, throwing up to heaven great fountains of water. I carefully noted the general effect. The land and sky were joined and on the water side the sea presented a strange spectacle; the crests of the waves formed little shadows and the sea appeared like an immense white, newly plastered wall. The ships moved like flies on a blue-green carpet, and left behind them a trail of white foam and an oily wake. A half-turn, and we were again over the open sea.

"Let's drop a couple of bombs on those boats, will you, la Burthe?" said I, pointing in their direction.

"Fine idea; we are high enough," he said; "our comrades are already far off, and the six Boches are following us along. Don't hesitate—just drop the bombs without going down."

Another half-turn and we had turned the nose of the machine into the wind, and just at the proper instant I let go one after the other. The result was doubtful, although they struck inside of fifty yards from the boats.

"Good! splendid!" said la Burthe; "there'll be surely some damage."

Upon our return, we fell in with some English scouting planes on the way to take a shot at the Boches.

"That looks good," I thought ; "they are evidently after big game."

We reached our starting-place without any loss of time, and with my memory fresh I painted what I had just witnessed.

The meals in our little shack were not very lively. The commandant, who sometimes posed as a wag, was naturally a little taciturn. A suggestion, a remark, or an order could be heard from time to time interrupting the monotonous noise of the knives

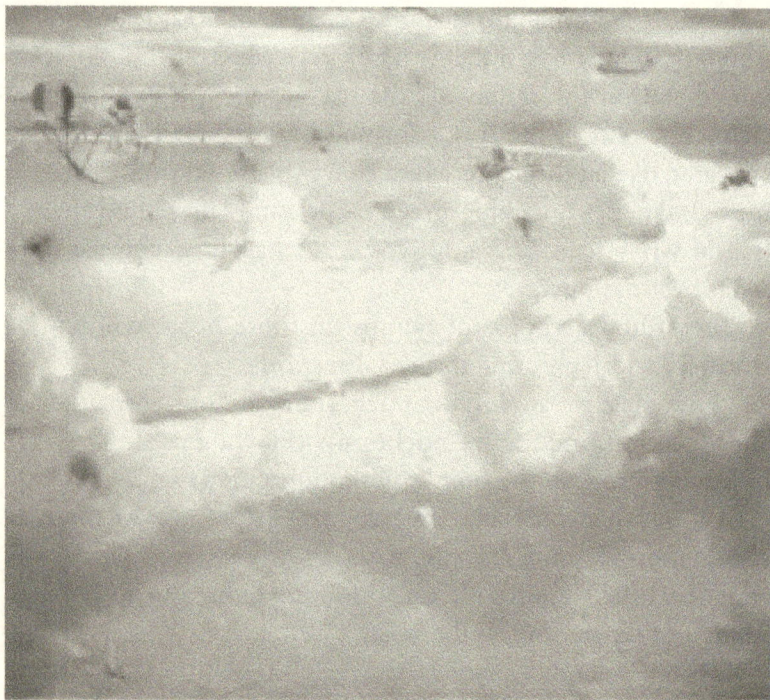

BOMBARDMENT OF THE MOLE AND
PORT OF ZEEBRUGGE, 1916

and forks on the plates, as no officer dared to disturb the meditations of the chief unless on official business.

"By Jove," said I, "I don't come from round here, and I am not accustomed to these protracted silences, which sometimes last throughout a meal. I can't make out the Commandant either. When I formerly knew him he was an entirely different man, overflowing with good-nature."

It happened that de la Morlaix sat next to him; they got into conversation through the efforts of the latter.

However, I put these conditions down to the role he played as chief, and to the shyness of his subordinates. I determined to broach the subject to him, and one day said to him suddenly, "Commandant, excuse me for breaking the silence. When conversation lags, will you permit me to start it up again?"

This sudden sortie made him laugh, for he perfectly understood my meaning. Retaining his sunny smile, he said to me, "I ask nothing better. It is the company, in spite of myself, that keeps me in a reflective mood." Everybody protested, but the ice was broken.

"Commandant," I said, "I will presently show you yesterday's bombardment of Zeebrugge, and I would like very much to have your opinion of it and the opinion of these gentlemen."

"What!" he exclaimed; "is it done already?"

"Yes, sir, and I hope you have some other subjects for me; I must divide my time between so many of them."

"Oh, yes, there are plenty, both tragic and comic subjects— like that of Routier, for example."

"That," said la Burthe, "is perfect! His arrival without a stitch of clothes on was simply fierce!"

"May I ask if it is possible for me to have the log-book?" I said.

"Most certainly," said the commandant, "but you will not find any touch of humour in the log."

"I'm sorry, but in that case. Commandant, won't you kindly tell us about it?"

"It is not absolutely a war story, but it is comic and tragic at the same time; as tragic as any that you will find in the log-book, and as truly interesting.

"In returning from the bombardment of Ostend, the stalling of the engine obliged him to come down, and there he was in mid-ocean. He examined his engine in company with his observer, to find out what the trouble was, and was tossed about roughly by the waves, when he suddenly saw, about six yards from him, a round, compact, dust-coloured mass, the size of a barrel.

"'What's that?' he said to his observer. 'That's a Boche floating mine, my dear sir, nothing more nor less,' answered the observer.

"'My God! We are gone—the wind is blowing us down on it—a collision, and goodbye to the chickens of Dunkerque!'

"'Ah, not yet!' said Routier, 'I would sooner lose my good name.'

"He undressed as quickly as he could—and you can imagine how quickly—and jumped overboard; it was certainly time. As gently as you would lead a lady in a dance, he towed away the frightful machine with one hand, and with the other he pushed off the plane.

"'Ouf!' he said, when he saw the small space between the mine and the plane growing larger through his efforts.

"It was very warm, and after regaining his hydroplane, just as if nothing had happened, he flew back to base, and forgot all about dressing himself. It was Sunday afternoon. The wife of the admiral, accompanied by two young ladies, had come to make a visit, they wanted to see the hydroplanes, and the arrival of the expedition if they were in time to do so. I knew that Routier had not returned, and I became considerably uneasy on his account, for he was due about half an hour before.

"We went down on the quay, and lining up on the edge of it we waited for the hydroplane, which was seen approaching. Routier came down, sprang out, and advanced towards us, but when he got within fifty yards, he stopped and appeared turned to stone. I called him and told him to come on closer. He an-

110

swered only by motions, which I could not understand. Tired of
this sort of conversation, I jumped into a little boat and found
him as nature made him. I was bursting with laughter, and he
told me his tale in a few words.

"I took the ladies off to my office and gave him time to get
out and dress himself, but he would not be presented."

"But the ladies," said I.

"They laughed like mad," he said. "He was a wonderful type,
and one of the best marksmen I have ever known. It is a pity
that you did not arrive fifteen days sooner; he would have told
you the tale himself."

"Has he gone ?" I asked.

"Yes; I sent him as an instructor to the base at St. Raphael,
near Nice."

"But you tell the story well. Commandant, I must say."

"I believe that it was after the bombardment of Zeebrugge;
here is a log of it. It was another one of those rotten stallings
which made the trouble. The weather was bad and the sea rough.
I discovered Routier on the water, not far from shore—about
five miles, perhaps—tossed about on the waves, quietly repairing
his motor. Suddenly the noise of a motor aroused him from his
work, and a Boche land-plane was seen approaching at about
fifty yards up.

"The observer jumped to his gun and cast it loose. 'Damn—
it is out of order!' he cried.

"'Oh, hell!' said Routier, 'jump out of that and pass me my
revolver.' The enemy jeered at him and hoisted his tri-colour,
then passed beyond, discharging his machine gun as he went.

"Routier fired only once. The plane returned and bore down
upon the unfortunate disabled one. This attack was renewed
four times, but the fourth time it was fatal, at least to the enemy
observer. With half his body out of the machine he got a bullet
in the head and fell backward. His firing ceased, of course, and
the Boche pilot took flight, carrying off with him the corpse of
his comrade."

"That 's a fine subject for a picture," I said; "I am going to

EXPLOIT OF PILOT ROUTIER, MARITIME AVIATION OF DUNKERQUE

begin it this afternoon."

"As you wish. The plane is in the hangar now. Would you like me to put it overboard?"

"What kind of weather was it?"

"Precisely like today."

"In that case, Commandant, I certainly would."

CHAPTER 13

Sea-Aviators

The dangers of sea-aviators are not exactly like those of the land, but at least they are more plentiful. When a land-plane is obliged to come down, it lands upon solid ground. I mean that when it is safely landed, all danger is over for it. It is easy then to get something to eat and to return to one's squadron by railroad, automobile, or any other convenient method, leaving the plane behind.

But it is another story with hydroplanes; the danger is increased to almost a fatal extent. A hydroplane lost in the mist or coming down in the open sea, whether from stalling or from lack of gas, has a chance if the sea is smooth and the base can be notified by carrier pigeons to send a destroyer, which perhaps will arrive in time to rescue the aviator before he is swamped and the plane is knocked to pieces in the sea.

A man could remain probably forty-eight hours on the surface of a calm sea, but if there is the slightest leak, his life is very short; his machine soon fills with water and sinks before aid arrives.

Another danger which is especially feared is to be rescued by enemy ships and made prisoner, or worse by a submarine, which seizes one and makes one follow the enemy mission and cruise with him, confined in the hold, across and through the mine-infested and patrolled waters.

The accompanying picture represents a case of this kind, where two hydroplanes were sunk and the aviators rescued by a destroyer which arrived just in time. These two hydroplanes were searching for mines which it was thought were planted by the enemy along our coasts and in front of our ports. Such mines sometimes break away and become very dangerous to navigation. At low water they often float awash and show a bulk about one meter in diameter. They are quite visible to aviators when flying very low.

In the course of one of these expeditions, one of the planes was obliged to come down and his companion continued his work; but seeing his comrade remain still on the water, he decided to go to his aid, and flew down, alighting alongside of him.

Suddenly the weather changed, a strong wind sprang up and the sea came up with it, until finally the observer was obliged to throw himself into the water and climb aboard the hydroplane in distress.

"What's the matter with it?"

"I'm sure I can't tell; it simply won't start."

"Good Lord! look at the water—is your engine going all right?"

"Yes, let's hurry up, old man; throw me your line and tow me; are we some distance offshore?"

"About twenty-five kilometres at least."

"What do you say—had we better loose some pigeons first?"

"I think so; that is more prudent; that is, unless we decide to remain here forever."

The four little birds took their messages, circled up in the air for about two minutes, and then struck out straight for land in search of help. By this time the sea had risen decidedly and the two planes were occasionally knocking into each other violently, and at times touched the water with their wings; the motor of one of them was still going.

The observer in the first machine climbed aboard his machine and endeavoured to get near enough to heave the tow-line, so as to tow the other ashore as one would tow a broken-down

HYDROPLANE AIDING ANOTHER IN DISTRESS,
MARITIME AVIATION, DUNKERQUE, 1916

motor. It was an almost impossible procedure on account of the rough sea, for there was great danger of a collision between the planes, which would certainly result in the loss of one if not both of them. The observer left his place and climbed out cautiously on the end of his machine in the effort to make fast the line, but the waves always tossed them apart at just the moment when he was about to be successful; they tried two, three, four times—impossible.

They began to despair, as the water commenced to fill the machine. The first plane was already awash and nearly swamped, so that it appeared to be only a question of time when it would sink for good. The other plane was unable to take the air, for the waves tossed it in such a manner as to risk its being crushed to bits against a neighbouring wave, if it tried to rise; but even if they had been able to, they would never have been reconciled to letting their comrades perish alone.

Finally it began to rain, with no sign of abatement in the weather. The sky was black and the clouds came down almost into the water. It was impossible to see more than two hundred yards, and, in short, they were in for very bad weather. Some destroyer would surely come to their help, but would it discover them? The message carried by the pigeons gave exactly their latitude, but would they allow for drift, wondered the poor unfortunates? They managed to keep up and to float about twenty yards apart.

" Well, my friends, this is the finish," said the pilot of the first plane; "our machine is full of water and we are slowly going down."

"All right, come on over to us, then, and we will sink together. Let us risk everything to gain everything. My engine is still going, and I will try to get nearer. Climb out on the end of your wing and seize mine if you can."

Assisted by his machine and also by the condition of the sea, which moderated for a moment, the two machines came together and remained in touch like two squirrels, so that the two men passed from the one into the other.

"Yes, but we are not safe yet," said one of them; "look at our machine—our poor old bus. It is gone for good."

As a matter of fact it was really at its last gasp, and it slowly sank into the depths of the sea. Here were four men all together in this frail shell of a hydroplane, in the midst of a gale of wind in mid-ocean. Just put yourself for a moment in their place, and remember that these men know what dangers they have to go through every time they start on one of these expeditions, that they are always and entirely at the mercy of a simple accident to the machine, and that succour cannot be counted upon.

Night soon began to fall, but the sea did not abate, and besides, as there was no more gasoline, the hydroplane became merely a dead weight on the water and was tossed about at the mercy of the waves. As a last hope they loosed three more pigeons, carrying a report of their position and drift.

"All right, boys," said one of the men. "Those who are hungry ought to go to sleep; I will keep watch. We must keep up our spirits." He was right; and in about a half-hour the silhouette of a destroyer came out of the darkness and gloom.

"Fire the machine gun," said one.

That was a sufficient signal. They were soon discovered, hauled aboard, and saved! It was time, for the second plane had taken in so much water that, before they got clear of it, it disappeared in its turn; it was impossible to save it.

CHAPTER 14

Torpedoing A Submarine

Hydroplanes also have the task of destroying by bombing any hostile force they may encounter—ships, submarines, railroad stations, factories, anything and everything that the enemy possesses on the coast, in his ports, or at sea.

There are a number of appliances for bomb releasing, but the best aid in the air, as it is on shore, is the skill which comes from experience. The accompanying picture shows an attack upon a submarine and its destruction. Hydroplanes usually carry two heavy bombs, suspended one on each side of the fuselage, within easy reach of the observer; in addition some planes are armed with a navy 37 mm. machine gun.

When the sea is comparatively smooth, a submerged submarine is quite visible to the naked eye, and appears as a dark body in the midst of a more transparent space.

During a search for mines a hydroplane surprised a Boche submarine in the North Sea, its periscope showing. Descending to a height of fifty meters, the aviator let go his two bombs, one after the other; the first struck about two yards forward of the periscope, and the second a few meters farther aft. A terrific explosion resulted, which threw a column of water and smoke to a height of fifty yards, and would have swamped the plane if it had remained stationary.

In order to get the result of this attack, the flyers circled along the foaming water, waiting for the commotion produced by the explosion to calm down, and then they saw debris of all kinds rise to the surface. A metallic, oily patch spread out over the sea, forming a large, greasy stain.

"One less," said the flyers; "if it could only be like this every day, submarine warfare would soon be a thing of the past. Alas, it is rare game, not always within reach of the bombs of hydroplanes."

At St. Pol, near Dunkerque, there was located the camp of a night bombarding squadron, and from secret reports we learned one bright day that some Zeppelins were moored at the entrance to the canal at Zeebrugge. It was a good night's work when a squadron of planes (Voisin) joined in a raid, and let fall on one objective—which was so well illuminated—more than one hundred bombs. We learned the result by snapshot photographs taken the first thing on the following day by our hydroplanes. These showed the two Zeppelins, which had been ready to start on a raid against the English coast, entirely destroyed, and this without any loss on our side except the one hundred bombs.

The service of photography took on from day to day a greater importance, especially to maritime aviation; and Commandant de Laborde wished to develop it still further by placing in charge of it a very active and able sergeant. Petty Officer Malville. During my stay there I made his acquaintance, but had to leave without seeing him again. He had received orders to photograph Zeebrugge and its coast defences. The expeditionary force was made up as usual of four planes, which were to protect him in case of trouble during his work. Lieutenant de Vaisseau de Salins was his pilot. All went well until the arrival at Zeebrugge.

An hour later three of the escort planes returned; the fourth—that is to say, Malville and his pilot—was missing. A quarter of an hour's grace is always allowed to late ones, because it sometimes happens that after their mission is accomplished, they take a little sail above the clouds, where everything is so divinely beautiful, particularly towards evening.

Half an hour passed and still no news. The chief of the pigeon service was notified, and he arranged an apparatus on his landing-platform for the pigeons, in such a way that, when the bird alighted, an electric circuit was made which rang a bell, when an attendant opened the door, and took the message and the messenger.

We did not wait very long; the bell soon rang, and the following message was received by the commandant:—

"After our mission was accomplished we were attacked by three enemy hydroplanes—we fought as long as we could, and until our engine was struck, when we came down."

Ten minutes later some more pigeons arrived with another message:—

"We are floating in the water under guard of a Boche hydroplane."

Five minutes later another:—

"The enemy destroyer has just arrived and we are prisoners, safe and sound. Look out for my wife and children, and notify the family of Lieutenant de Salins. Signed, Malville, de Salins."

I saw Malville three months afterwards on a leave of absence of seven days at Paris. I was more than astonished upon opening my door to find myself face to face with him, and thought I saw a ghost.

"Well, how did you ever get here?" I asked.

"By escaping—simple enough," he replied.

"That 's all right, but how?"

"Simplest way in the world—in the clothes of a Boche soldier and with a leave pass. The only difficulty was at the frontier; there I had real trouble." Then he told me a tale which I regret very much that I cannot now repeat.

"What do you propose to do?" I asked him.

"Return to Dunkerque; of course, as soon as my report to the Minister of Foreign Affairs is made."

"And de Salins?"

"Ah, I don't know; we weren't in the same camp."

"Oh, well, old man, let 's have dinner together, will you?"

"What did you think when you saw that we didn't come

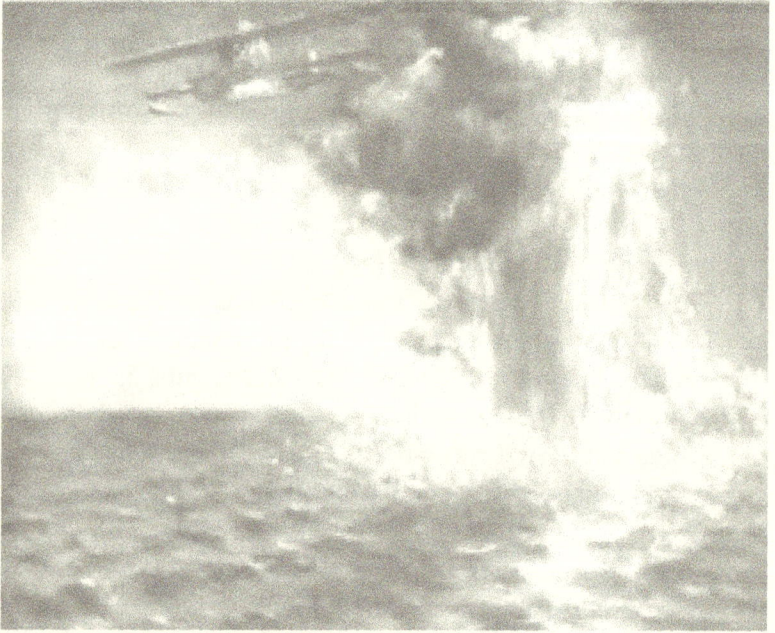

BOMBARDMENT OF AN ENEMY SUBMARINE BY AN
F.B.A. HYDROPLANE, NORTH SEA, 1916

back?"

"What do you suppose we thought! We imagined everything up to the time of the arrival of the three messages. A destroyer was all ready to leave for your rescue, but naturally didn't shove off."

"What did the Commandant have to say to the three others who served as escort?"

"He was white with rage; he didn't dare to open his mouth for a week. He certainly had something to be angry about, for if you had never come back, it would have been their fault."

"Oh, yes, one against three is too much. We fought one to three for a quarter of an hour at least. One of the three Boches was wounded, but our radiator was struck and we had to come down."

"And your Boche comrades—did they treat you well?"

"Very well; they questioned us separately, and when they found we had nothing to say, they did not insist, and we passed the night in their mess. After dinner we drank champagne, real champagne at that. I think they do that sort of thing in the hope that we will treat them the same way when we take them prisoners."

I had spent about a month with these robbers of the sea, so that on my departure my professional baggage was of some size. I had produced twenty studies and had collected much manuscript, all of which delighted de Laborde.

"Choose one for yourself," I said.

"No!—do you really mean it? What will the museum say?"

"Oh, one more or less makes no difference," I said; and then he took one of those representing his fighting plane flying over the sea.

"This will be my finest war souvenir," he said.

He was not to keep it very long, for about eight days later the hangars burnt down, destroying all that they contained.

I was pleased enough with them, but not quite with the finish. I have already given the reason for this, for like the Wandering Jew, I keep moving, following the changes in methods and putting them down day by day. "Later on, you can really make some works of art," I said to myself; "that is, let 's hope you will have the ability to do so."

CHAPTER 15

At Cachy

I was about half through with my work, but I judged that the worst half still remained: aviation schools, fighting aviation, and the portraits of aviators who became distinguished during the war.

After leaving Dunkerque, I stopped at Amiens, and took advantage of being there to telephone Captain Féquant, who commanded a group of scouting planes, in which was incorporated the already famous *Lafayette Escadrille.*

"Hello."

"Hello."

"Captain Féquant?"

"Yes."

"This is Farré, Captain. Can you come and get me? I want to spend a few days with you."

"Well, this is a pleasure; certainly. I am going to the Staff Head-quarters tomorrow at ten o'clock. You be there, and I will take you off to Cachy, where we are now."

I was very glad, indeed, to see him again, and he recalled to me the old V.B. 101 that he had commanded after Lieutenant Mouchard, at the great bombardments of Nancy.

"Whenever I see you, I always think of my poor brother and of the portrait you made of him on his deathbed."

"You still have no desire to give it to the Army Museum, have you?"

"Oh, never. I sent it to his wife with your compliments, and she wouldn't give it up for anything in the world."

"I scarcely like to laud my own work. I did it on watch with de la Morlaix. I was fairly well pleased with it; it was probably the emotion of the moment which inspired me."

"It is a truly remarkable inspiration and is a striking resemblance; for us, of course, it is priceless. It is a holy relic for my poor sister."

His eyes were dimmed with tears at the thought. I took him by the arm and changed the conversation, and carried him off to his automobile.

"Is Cachy far from here?" I asked.

"No, about twenty minutes."

"Tell me. Captain, have you really the *Lafayette Escadrille* in your command?"

"Yes, I still have it."

"Are you pleased with it?"

"Oh, they are splendid—a most devoted lot. Just think, those young men give up everything for their country, their youth, their blood; I most certainly am proud to be their commander."

"Are Lufbery and Thaw here now? I shall probably go to America, and I should be sorry not to have their portraits to show to their compatriots."

"Too late today; it is eleven o'clock, but tomorrow I'll invite them to luncheon and introduce them to you."

"I also want to make a portrait of you, if you can arrange it."

"Why, yes, but on condition you do it right away, because I leave the day after tomorrow by order of the quartermaster-general."

"Is Brocard also at Cachy?"

"Yes, he is there. The sector is divided between us, and we do good work; and the Boches don't get much of a chance."

We had now arrived, and as on all such occasions, I found old friends and made some new ones. De Kerillis was also there with his famous *escadrille* of Caudron bi-motors; the same one that bombarded Karlsruhe with such great success, killing about six hundred, and about the same number at Nancy.

I remember so well their departure; the machines were so heavy with gasoline and shells that they could hardly leave the ground. It was one of those reprisal raids which made the Boche pay dearly for his crimes at Bar-le-duc. Of nine planes, two remained prisoners after a terrific fight at a height of four thousand meters, when they were engaged against twelve Boches.

Another bombardment, of Absheim, led by Commandant Happe, the one that they called—for I have heard that he did not like to hear it—the pirate of the air, was almost like it, but with a difference.

Commandant Happe was certainly the most terrible adversary that ever French aviation had employed; very tall, with a brown beard, reserved, and without the slightest care for personal safety; on the contrary, the only charge that might be made against him was temerity; but it is hard to reproach a chief who sets a good example—who takes the lead in every expedition at the head of his group.

"It is war," he said to me; "we must keep on continually killing the Boches, for the dead are the ones who never return to fight again."

Every occasion to do this was a good one for him. If during a flight he made out a railroad train, he came down immediately and headed directly for it. Flying low at a level with the windows of the cars, he poured a fusillade from his machine gun into the occupants. He attacked military trains only, and always drew off if he caught sight of a woman or a child among them.

In bombarding expeditions, as I have already said, the setting-out and the fighting can be done with sufficient safety; it is only on the return that the exposure is great and an engagement almost inevitable. That of was a terrible example. Captain X, an Argentine volunteer, a pilot before the war, of great bravery and absolute self-forgetfulness, gave me an account of it.

They had left Luxeuil, near Belfort. After a successful bombardment of the city, there were thirty of them in all returning,

WILLIAM THAW

when they fell in with about forty Boche planes and attacked them at once. It was magnificent! It lasted ten minutes; air battles are always soon over. Just imagine these fighters flying at a speed of one hundred miles a minute! At last a dozen of them on each side were seen to fall; some in flames, others with tanks exploding; it was a grand display of fireworks.

Ten minutes later there remained no visible trace of that terrible meeting of men in the regions of the eagle, except perhaps a few faint, dark streaks of smoke, that faded away on the breath of a light breeze. It was the most famous air battle of the war, and if it was so fearful, it was because each enemy knew his adversary, and ardently wished to destroy him at any price, or to capture him. The Boches were so desirous of getting Happe that they had set a price on his head.

While talking of these adventures with the captain, the hour for luncheon arrived, and I was now a little late for it. Thaw and Lufbery were already there. These two men represented two very different types; Thaw was refined, distinguished-looking, with a certain sweetness of manner: he commanded the *Lafayette Escadrille*. He was, like Lufbery, one of the first American aviators, and the entire escadrille was made up of his compatriots; men who professed a deep admiration and love for France; and who—among the very first—voluntarily and spontaneously answered the call of Lafayette, and said, "We are not many, but our example will bear fruit. The soil of America is so fertile that for every grain planted in that land of liberty, there will be produced hundreds of thousands."

This prophecy is today accomplished, and it was Pershing, who before the tomb of Lafayette announced it in those simple words, "We are here"; and he also announced it to the Boches of Saint-Mihiel by the noise of his cannon and the spirit of his soldiers! Glory be to all the heroes of the *Lafayette Escadrille*, to which belongs the honour of first shedding American blood on the altar of Liberty.

From the date of its organization. Thaw commanded that fighting squadron, whose exploits, both of individuals and in general, have been most remarkable; it occupies a place in the minds of our men far above the average of our fighting squadrons. Its pilots have each received their *Croix de Guerre*; each of them has brought down several adversaries; Thaw has downed his eighth, and Lufbery, whose French friends familiarly called him *l'oeuf* (the Egg), fell, alas, his glorious task incomplete, after twenty-one victories.

His physiognomy shone with loyalty—his clear look, with the blue of steel, gave an impression of great promptness and decision. He was lively and energetic; but his nose, slightly flattened on his face, suggested a thoroughbred courier of the air, and his jaw great material force under the control of an indomitable will.

His death, like that of Guynemer,—without at all resembling that in manner,—was a deeply tragic one; like a cherished child of God, Minerva seemed to have surrounded him with her protection. In his last fight his adversary set him afire; at once he planed to earth, with the evident intention of landing before being destroyed by the flames. The length of this flight must have been too great, for at hardly three hundred yards from the ground, he was seen to throw himself out of his plane, and fall into a bed of flowers. His fall was fatal. They picked him up insensible from among the roses and the laurels, which seemed to weep over him.

Back to Paris—and after having turned over to General Niox, director of the Army Museum, my pictures on maritime aviation, I went to call on an under-secretary of aviation, my friend Captain Maurice, whom I had known when he was a member of the First Bombarding Group.

"Well, Farré, when are you coming to us? It is very important for our schools and for history as well, as everything will practically disappear after the war. These are worth a great deal, and besides, a careful record should be made of them for history's sake."

"Whenever you like Captain."

"Would you like me to tell Colonel Girod to order you to

the Department?"

"Why—yes—I would."

"Well, that 's all right; you can go in peace now, but not for very long; in two days you may expect orders."

"And the Quartermaster-General?"

"Oh, it does not matter about the Quartermaster-General, as long as you are ordered by the Department."

I went immediately. Taking a list of schools and a map, I planned my tour of France; this expedition in the peace zone scarcely suited me; it would require at least three months to do everything, and three months' absence from the front would be a little difficult to make up. Go on, old Wandering Jew, trot along; and I made up my list.

First Chartres; then Ambérieux, near Lyons; Miramas; Yetres, near Marseilles; Pau in the Pyrenees; Gazeaux, school for aerial marksmanship near Bordeaux, and return to Paris. Afterward Avor, an important school furnishing two hundred pilots a month; Tours, Châteauroux, Vineuil, Issoudun for the Americans, were then scarcely planned and did not yet exist.

I was accompanied by an officer whose duty it was to make a report upon any emplacement selected. I did not neglect Etampes, Juvisy, and Buc, all three in the suburbs of Paris; Issy, also, and les Moulineaux, our great manufacturing centre. Forty studies was the result of this trip, and I was anxious to return again to the front.

RAOUL LUFBERY

CHAPTER 16

With The Stork Escadrille

My friend, Commandant Brocard, under whose orders the famous Stork Escadrille was operating, was then at Manoncourt, near Nancy. My group was there too, but I had not yet asked for new orders; but on announcing my arrival by telephone the next day, I found myself among these formidable fighters. Ah, how nice they seemed; they had nothing arrogant or malicious about them: Lieutenant Heurtaux, almost a boy; the distinguished Deullin, who regarded me with curiosity; the lively Captain Auger and the reserved Père Dorme, calm as deep water; the street urchin Raymond, always content; Fonck, who was just beginning to distinguish himself, and who had already passed in number the victories of Guynemer; de la Tour, who was at the hospital taking care of his jaundice; Lieutenant Duval—and in fact, the entire crowd.

Guynemer was not there; he arrived some days afterwards. All these officers were lodged in an immense farmhouse that they called the *château* as a joke, because it was the largest in the village.

"Ah, here you are. Goodmorning, old chap."

"Commandant, I want to thank you for taking me into the bosom of your formidable family."

"To take you in is very easy for me, but to find you a lodging is difficult. How long do you expect to remain?"

"Upon my word, sir, I don't know—fifteen days—three weeks—months; it will depend upon these gentlemen."

"They are a very good lot, but it will be hard for you to get them to pose for you. Look at them first—gain their confidence—they are already disgusted with several of your colleagues, who were not very successful, however, and that makes them rather suspicious."Then, turning towards his secretary,"Say, Tournier, our house is full, isn't it?"

"As full as an egg. Commandant," replied Tournier.

"Where the devil can we lodge our friend Farré?"

"I'll take care of that, sir."

"Great—I have an idea; go and find Monsieur le Cure. I remember he told me that he could spare me a room. Run and see if it is still at my disposal.

"Curses! That telephone again—I would like to blow it to bits.

"Hello, this is Commandant Brocard! Yes!

"What is it?

"An enemy squadron—where?

"I can't hear.

"Over Nancy?

"Well, what kind of planes?

"What's that?

Bombarding—in what direction?

"Due north?"

Then he wrote the following order:

"Squadron No. 3, a group of four bombarding planes coming from the north are directed towards Nancy. Four fighting planes will immediately prepare to meet them." He added the following postscript:"De Billy will please communicate this to Lieutenant Heurtaux, commanding the Third Escadrille, for immediate execution."

Tournier was just returning. "Well, what did that dear old *curé* say?"

"He says he is waiting for Monsieur Farré, Commandant; a room is at his disposition."

"Oh, that's splendid! Please excuse me; I have piles of papers on my desk as high as my head! Make yourself comfortable and remember that you are in your own house; we have luncheon at noon."

It was then eleven o'clock, and I made use of a moment's leisure to pay a call on the cure, and to take possession of my room.

It was now February, 1917, and the weather very damp and cold at night; it had already frozen solid and hardened the thick mud of the roads.

Today was balmy and exhilarating, but at midday, in passing over to the castle where these gentlemen messed, I had to cross a swamp where the mud had been thawed out by the sun.

The commandant placed me on his right, and Captain Auger alongside of me. What a difference from Dunkerque—quite the reverse here, for sometimes three, four conversations kept pace with the noise of the mess service; Father Dorme said nothing.

"Well, gentlemen," said the commandant, "what is the result of your expedition this morning?"

"Oh, Commandant, I forgot—a telephone message was received a moment ago, during your absence, from the Twenty-eighth Division, saying that a Boche bombarding plane fell in flames in the Forest of Pont-à-Mousson."

"I brought it down, sir," cried Captain Auger; "I did not wish to mention it to you before the news had been confirmed."

"Idiot, why not?"

"Dorme struck one down himself at Lunéville, but it is not yet confirmed," said Lieutenant Heurtaux.

"Look at Father Dorme," said the commandant in a low voice to me; "he never says much, but he is my best help. He doesn't say a word when anything like this happens. As soon as he lands, he takes off his teddy-bear, changes his helmet for a cap,—which his mechanic always has ready for him,—takes his cane, and goes to his office; makes his report without any superfluous words, and then goes for a walk. He is certainly a character; look at that head; I would give a good bit to see him with a fishing-line in his hand near some creek—wouldn't you?"

"I think he is rather disconcerting."

"Well, of all my pilots, he and Heurtaux are the best."

"Oh, Guynemer,—that's another thing."

"Where do you get your pilots. Commandant? Do they send them to you from the rear, or can you choose them?"

"Principally from the rear. I usually know something of the pilots who ask to come, or if I don't, I am guided more or less by the opinions of one of these chaps; and if by chance I draw a weak brother—somebody I don't know—and if he has cold feet, he will not tarry here very long. He will ask of his own accord to change. As you see, it is like a real family."

"Yes, it is a perfectly happy mess," I said, "with such a chief and such men; it is ideal. One of the greatest qualities of a chief is to promote harmony among his subordinates; be dignified, and make himself loved and respected by setting a good example."

"Yes, that's very true, and the whole thing in a nutshell."

"Commandant, you remind me, by your amiable qualities and even by your physical appearance, of a great friend of mine that I have lost—Lieutenant Mouchard."

"Ah, you knew him!—a fine fellow; what a sublime death he suffered."

"Oh, wonderful, beautiful!"

"Were you there?"

"Yes; if he had let me, I should have been with him. He did not sacrifice his life in vain, for how many night bombardments have been made since he led the way!"

The postman arrived and we went over the mail with our coffee.

About one hundred letters arrived here for the fifteen officers. Tournier distributed the mail.

"Heurtaux, here's something for you—Deullin—Raymond, that's from your little friend. What's the matter with you!"

"Be a little more respectful," said Raymond, laughing.

"Guynemer, Guynemer, always Guynemer!"

"Oh, he's a sad man with his mail; there's never anything except for him," cried Auger; "he seems to be the real thing."

"Auger, here's something for you—stop crying," said Tournier.

"Ah, that's fierce luck—from my father; haven't you any others?" asked Auger.

"Tomorrow, old dear. Dorme not here? Where is he? He doesn't hang around here much!"

"Ah, yes, one for the chief; one that smells good. Those from the Quartermaster-General have no smell. Here's a package too, sir!"

"Let's see the package; that's what most interests me."

Upon opening it we found, carefully wrapped together, as many handkerchiefs as there were pilots in Squadron No. 3.

"Ah, she seems to be pretty well informed—this lady."

They were beautifully embroidered by hand with a stork, which was the emblem of the squadron, and a card accompanied them.

"Who is it? Who is it?" cried Auger curiously.

"You shut up!"

To Commandant Brocard, commanding Group No. 2 of Fighting Planes. Commandant, permit me, as an admirer of your heroes, to offer this homage to their valour.

(Signed)   X

"Here is something that the observation squadrons never receive," said I to the commandant.

"Ah, the unfortunates! I should say not!"

In the afternoon, everyone went about his business and joined his squadron to go out hunting Boches and to go over his plane. All of them, or nearly all of them, went in the Spad, the very latest invention of an engineer named Béchereau; it was a wonderful machine and really very superior in design to all other fighting planes. Nevertheless, the Nieuport was still preferred by some pilots, who found it more handy.

The afternoon was fine and the sun warm, and I said to myself, "I will take advantage of it, for if it rains tomorrow, goodbye to my studies, for fine days are very rare at this season of the year."

Taking my painting gear, I went down to the camping

grounds, carrying with me something to sit on and something for an easel; usually three cans of gasoline—one to sit on, and the others placed on top of each other made a very fine easel. Guynemer was not there, but his plane was, and pulling it out of the hangar and placing it in a position for taking flight, I made a drawing of it, in order to familiarize myself with its shape, which was still new to me. The greater part of the pilots gathered around me, except Raymond. I had just finished my study when a plane came down.

"Ah, that's Auger; I know him by the way he lands—splendid pilot."

"Good style, too, hasn't he?" said I.

"Oh, yes."

It turned out to be really he.

"Well, old man, what do you suppose I did over Frouart? I had a little run over the course with four Boches. Oh, those rotters! They just barely failed to get me too! Look here,"—and he showed me a rip in the leather of his vest.

"But you are wounded, old man."

"No; it's only the skin of my coat."

"But I tell you it is your own—look here,"—and putting his finger into the tear, he drew it out dripping with blood.

"Oh, by Jove, that's too much." He took off his coat and exposed a furrow in his skin, the whole length of one side.

"That's fierce; I never felt it; I mean to say I did feel a little shock, but I didn't believe the bullet had struck. My pocket-book—what's happened to it?—shot through and through!" and he pulled out a package of one hundred *franc* bank-notes, shot through.

"Oh, a fine souvenir; I must have one," I said.

"All right, old chap, that 's one hundred *francs*, even though there is a history to it."

"Thank you—you give me great pleasure," said I, offering him another brand-new one; "now one of your bank-notes is well again."

"Ah, that's the kind of a wound to have," he said, laughing.

"Do you think I can call this a regular war wound?"

"You must be crazy; of course you can as long as blood was shed."

"Now, old man, it was the other one whose blood was shed. I came down on him and I never left him. I wanted to catch him, you know, but he bore a charmed life, and in the midst of it I suddenly discovered the fire of four machine guns concentrated on me. But I was thinking of the other one; he will never need a wound certificate. The Commandant will be glad for my sake, for that makes my fifth—believe me—and I am now an Ace with a big A. Do you understand that—an Ace; do you know what that means?" He was crazy with joy. "What do you say to that? One this morning and one this evening. Where is the Commandant now?"

"Where would he be if not in his office?"

"Well, come along, and don't worry me. I have full right to be pleased now and to tell it to all the world, and I am going to do it."

He ran into the office and cried, "Old man, there it is; that makes the fifth. You must put me in the running for a citation this time."

"Lord, what a chatter! Keep quiet, will you?"

The commandant was telephoning the quartermaster-general; they were very old friends, and when they were together, the difference in rank made no difference in their friendship. He hung up the receiver.

"Are you sick, old man?"

"No, I'm not sick, but you have got to sign me a wound certificate all the same. Look!"

"You must go to the hospital; and what have you done, anyway?" said the commandant, chaffing him.

"I want to tell you again that I have just brought down another Boche, and that it is necessary for you to put me on the list for a citation. I am an Ace now with a big A; isn't that so, Raymond?"

"Patience, patience, my son; wait for the confirmation."

When a pilot has brought down his fifth plane, the chief of the squadron telegraphs his fifth victory to headquarters, and that gives him the right to be carried in the next general orders to the whole army with a citation of service rendered, for the press to publish the following day in the Official Gazette.

Whenever pilots merited this distinction, their machinists called them Aces, which has the same signification amongst the pilots as the ace card has in a game of cards; that is to say, the strongest card, and this is the etymology of the word "ace," of which many persons are ignorant. This title has nothing official, and it sprung from the slang of the machinists, but that does not prevent it from being quoted in all languages and in every country in the world.

Dear old Auger was my first model—with a surprising vivacity, always contented; he was the last word in good fellows among the squadron, and he shared a room with his old friend Heurtaux. From the time he turned out in the morning, he sang like a bird, giving imitations of an orchestra in a country fair playing all instruments at once. Too brave, too rash, he would never succeed in increasing very much the number of his victories, for every day he told of his fights against three, four, five Boches.

"Oh, I'm crazy, I know," he said, after listening to the advice of the commandant. "I know that they will get me in the end, but before I go, my dear friend, they will have to pay the price of my hide."

Six months later at Dunkerque, a little before the death of his comrade Guynemer, he was mortally wounded on the aerial field of battle, but had the strength left to bring his machine back to his squadron headquarters. His weakness, however, caused him to make a bad landing, and he tumbled. Running to his rescue, they pulled him out from under his machine; he had just died with a ball in his forehead after his seventh victory.

Already Lieutenant Dorme had preceded him among the heroes *dead on the field of honour*, and, like him, was killed in unequal combat. We knew it from the capture of an enemy aviator, in whose pockets we found his watch, in which was engraved his name—"To Father Dorme." The death of Lieutenant Dorme was a great enemy victory and a great loss for French aviation; with his calmness and grasp of tactics, he was one of the most daring pilots of the air.

Being in the spirit of it one day, he told me the story of one of his adventures.

"You know how I fly, don't you—never in a straight line. I go up or I descend; I turn to the left or right; I never give time for a Boche to surprise me; by doing this, I always have a chance to surprise them. This morning after one of my descents, I discovered one of them just above me. Oh, there he was, and he needed to be protected by the good God. I held him right where I wanted him for about ten minutes, at the end of my machine gun, until I made out what became of him and I saw him fall. I again pulled the trigger of my machine gun, but nothing happened; it was jammed. I tried to repair it, but nothing doing. I had to watch him speed off and was powerless to prevent his getting away. It was a lucky escape for him, let me tell you, and I am sure there would have been no doubt about it if my machine gun had not jammed."

"His time had not come," I replied; "and, as you say, his old *Gott* protected him."

Some days later I had the pleasure of seeing him in a different light. Guynemer had come back and brought with him his third captain's stripe and his cross of officer of the Legion of Honour. We decided to give him a good reception and to include in the honours Commandant Brocard, who had also got a promotion. It was the restaurant of *la Liégeoise*, formerly known as *la Viennoise*, which had the honour of gathering together in the evening, at a banquet, all the Aces of No. 2 Combat Group.

I remember very well the manner in which the great Chief of Aviation, Colonel Barrès, president, felicitated Guynemer.

"Look here, Guynemer," said he, "I remember you as a simple private; now you are captain. If you continue this speed, you will be a general before I am."

In the middle of the table there was placed a white stork, which was the emblem of No. 3 squadron. Dorme got hold of this and made it part of all his fantastic pranks during the rest of the evening. I have never seen a living being transform himself so rapidly, but I attributed it to the speedy disappearance of the first bottle of champagne.

At dessert I took one of the little French flags which ornamented the table and collected on it the signatures of all the principal heroes of the air present. Dear, precious little French flag; five of these signatures are already carried in the golden book of those who died for their country. I shall preserve it carefully.

After dinner, the party broke up and each one left in the automobile that had brought him. I found myself ensconced in that occupied by Dorme, Raymond, and Lieutenant de Vaisseau Nogrel.

"Look here, Father Dorme, we are not going to go home, are we?" said Raymond.

"Not on your life!" exclaimed Nogrel.

"My word, I want to go out bombarding tonight," said Dorme; "where is Boubouse?" (Boubouse was the driver of the car.)

"Don't worry about him, old man; there he is. He feels there's wind in the sails this evening—he is pleased enough, all right," answered Nogrel.

"Come here, Boubouse—look here, do you know Nancy?"

"Yes, sir."

"You must know where there is something open this time of night."

In the dusk of the evening his face was illuminated by a smile. He simply nodded his head, but this sign spoke worlds. I saw some fun ahead for that night, and wondered how I could get out of it. It was already ten o'clock; the city was dark; I had no carriage to get back to Manoncourt, which was at least fifteen kilometres away, and I objected timidly and with reason.

"You know, we have got to have special permission to run

around town at this hour of the night, and the general commanding this place has given us permission only until ten o'clock."

"Ah, Father Farré, don't hinder us. What's the matter with you? You are not going to hold us up in that way; why not have a little run? We may be smashing our heads off tomorrow—what?"

"What could I say to that?" I thought, and made no further remonstrance.

The next day, or rather the same morning, as the sun rose upon the horizon, it found them on the job and already in the air waiting for the awakening of the inhabitants of Nancy, for it was always in the early dawn that our Boche friends bombarded our good city of Nancy—and it was nothing new to have a few Boche planes in sight at luncheon.

CHAPTER 17

A Delightful Evening

The evening of the day following this feast, everyone felt the need of a little repose and rest, and all took themselves off home early. The prodigal son, Lieutenant de la Tour, almost thoroughly recovered in health, had again taken his place at mess, and, with his usual blithe spirits, entertained his comrades with much interesting conversation.

"Tell me, de la Tour, what are you doing around here, anyway?" said the commandant. "It seems to me that you have about three weeks of leave for your convalescence."

"Yes, Commandant, that's true, but if you don't mind, I won't take advantage of it, because for a long time I have not flown; everyone has brought down his German while I have been in the hospital, and I am very anxious to catch up."

"You are a pretty fierce subject; you want to be as good as Dorme. Now don't mistake me—I don't blame you; on the contrary, I think you show the right spirit."

"I simply want forty-eight hours' leave to go to Paris, Commandant," he said, laughing.

"Granted; I know why; go ahead!"

"And how about my mail?" said Guynemer.

"Ah, my good Captain,"—wasn't it perfectly disgusting to have to call this youngster Captain?—here, old man," said Captain Auger. "There you are, there's your mail."

Another hundred letters from almost all parts of the world except Germany were placed on the big table in the mess-room,

144

and there was a scramble as each one sorted out his own letters. There were some for everybody, but acting with discretion, I will simply say that the greater part of these very fine-looking letters proved beyond doubt the existence of sincere admirers— women, children, young girls and boys—fired with patriotism, showing their admiration for the new Chevalier Bayard. There were many requests for autographs made under one pretext or another; I may add that few received them.

At such times Lieutenant Heurtaux frequently furnished us music on a piano.

This evening was a delightful one for me. Usually the best flyers do not make up an artistic reunion. The subjects of their conversation are not varied, and aside from descriptions of their exploits, which they exchange with each other, they hardly afford me intellectual nourishment of a professional kind. However, with this crowd, it was somewhat different. All of these heroes, the oldest being not more than twenty-five years of age, were of good family, well educated, with good minds, and Commandant Brocard encouraged professional study among them.

"I should like very much indeed to hear them tell their tales," I said to the commandant. "How can I get them to do it?"

"That isn't easy to do; they are not very great talkers. De la Tour seems to be well disposed. I will try to start him on one of his fights. Look here, de la Tour, where were we when you brought down your last Boche, with two of his mates, all going down in flames?"

"That was on the Somme, Commandant."

"Tell us, will you, what happened? Farré wants to make a picture of it, which will be a great and interesting thing for history."

"Ah, Commandant, it isn't the custom of the Squadron to do that. I should bore these gentlemen."

"Oh, go ahead," said Auger; "we can stand it."

"It's an order, then."

"No, old man," replied Raymond with a wave of his hand. "It's a prayer—you speak so well."

I saw his embarrassment, and went over and took a seat near him, alongside of the stove; and while the conversation was renewed among the others, I listened to him.

"You remember our trip to Cachy, near Amiens, in the month of May, 1916. One day when it was raining torrents, you came to see the Commandant but soon went away. It was during the offensive of the Somme. By cricky, how many Boche planes were brought down at that time! We were really masters of the air! My fight occurred then, and it was the first time that I ever felt any emotion at the death of an enemy. Those five minutes of the drama made an indelible impression upon me.

"I left at sunrise one beautiful morning. The soft clouds in the heavens were very high, the atmosphere clear. I knew that the Boche only crossed the lines at an altitude varying between five and seven thousand meters. 'If I keep below them, I shall not encounter anything,' I thought.

"My motor was running beautifully; I felt that the machine could rise to any height. At about four thousand meters, I ran into a light bank of stratus clouds, which spread out horizontally and then vertically like a head of hair or a grove of weeping willows. Their colour, brought out by the rising sun, was golden, blue, mauve, and various other shades; another cloud a thousand meters higher was just the same.

"Still higher, the action of the sun produced a different effect. Clouds there resembled tufts of carded wool and formed golden lines, and stretched out at about the same height. After going above these clouds, I found myself between six and seven thousand meters high and no longer saw the earth, except through parts of clouds in which there were gaps. Above me there was nothing except the vaulted blue dome of heaven. I considered this a splendid point of view, and had the whole of that vast space to myself, for there was no enemy in sight, not even a black spot that might denote another plane.

"I flew to the right and to the left, made turns, and left no part of the heavens unsearched, until finally, as my machine took a rise, I made out a little black point. 'Ah, there's a comrade! Is it a true comrade or a false one?' I thought.

"'I will run over to him, anyway.' The distance that separated us then was about six kilometres and was rapidly diminishing. He had seen me, and evidently the same thought entered his head.

"I tested my machine gun; ta-ta-ta, going all right; I could count on that. You know, at such heights, the atmospheric pressure not being the same, the machine gun sometimes works badly or even stops. This is appalling when it happens in the presence of an adversary, who remains in good condition himself and brings you down without pity. We were now separated by only about fifteen hundred meters. I began to make him out. No doubt it was a Boche, and judging from his speed, a fighting plane.

"Three seconds later I could make out his model. It was an Albatross of most recent design—about the same form and quality as our Spad which I was piloting. By certain manoeuvres that he made I was able to size him up. 'Now,' said I to myself, 'just wait; that chap there has fire in his eye and is after your scalp. It is up to you to try to get his.'

"We passed each other several times; it was evident that he wished to catch me on the run; that is to say, to get in my dead angle, just behind me. The fighting qualities of our two machines were about equal, but nevertheless I seemed to have the advantage over him in speed; it was a fight between skilled tacticians.

"The action became hot and in earnest. I turned towards my foe; he did the same. I slowed down in order to turn better; as soon as he passed me, I veered rapidly and got in his wake. I opened my throttle and kept up the speed, never slacking an instant, when at about twenty meters from him, I saw him turn and look at me, knowing he was a dead man, whether he dived or whether he kept on straight.

"He swerved to the left and commenced to circle in order to get out of his position of danger, and into a position in my rear, but I was watching his every movement and held close to his stem, and then became involved in the manoeuvre of 'chas-

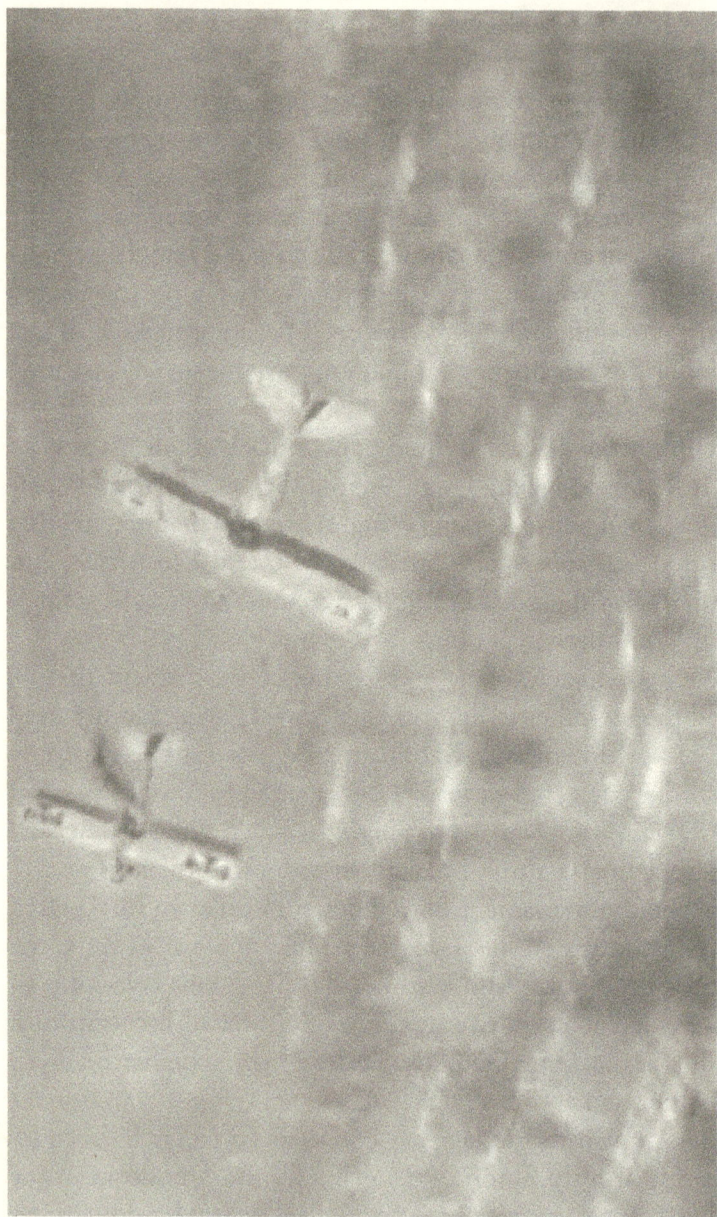

ing tails.' So we kept on turning for a time that seemed like a hundred years—he doing his best to keep out of the arc of fire of my machine gun and I trying to get him within it.

"Just once, for a moment only—not over two seconds—I had him 'on' with my gun-sights; I pressed the trigger. I saw my murderous shots strike him in vital parts—his machine wobbled—he was wounded or killed. He dropped down like a sinking ship, and fell through space like a dead leaf in autumn. I could not resist staying near him and spiralling downward with him.

"Our fight had lasted five minutes, and it was quite time it was over, for I saw two enemies approaching to succour their comrade. Being out of ammunition, I stopped my descent; the other two turned about fifteen hundred meters below me; I should be able to dodge them.

"The beaten adversary turned round and round in the air, falling slowly. A light trail of smoke followed his machine. Suddenly it burst into flames and fell to earth like an enormous torch, leaving behind it a heavy column of black smoke. His two comrades saw him fall, and ceasing their efforts to get near me, they commenced to turn in spiral descent around their lost comrade, with a view apparently to attending him in his terrible but glorious death.

"This produced a strong impression upon me. His death appeared to me to be most horrible. Perhaps, unconsciously, I thought how I should feel if I had been in his place."

"I don't think the Boche would have the same feeling regarding you," I said.

"That's very likely, and it was that thought which brought me to my senses about the fallen German!"

"That was a true aerial tournament between two adversaries, very fierce and very fine; but, it is not always that way."

"All except fighting planes are in great danger. Our scouting planes are not protected, and whenever any of them are attacked, seventy-five out of a hundred are brought down."

"Well, if you want to stop that, we have got to be masters of the air, and you fighting planes ought to realize that."

"You are absolutely right, Farré," said Guynemer, coming up at that moment. "Poor old observation bombarding planes—it is simply murder to bring them down. It is very rarely that one meets in the air an adversary of equal force in both strength and material. One cannot be expected to give quarter to machines that come over our lines. We should attack them at all hazards and with all our strength, whether it is in a sense gallant to do so or not, for the consequences are very great, indeed, when we consider our infantry and artillery; but in spite of right, there exists a natural repugnance to an unequal fight, for then we become simply assassins. When you come to think it over, they have no such pity for us, and you can't make me think otherwise.

"Tell me, as I am free tomorrow morning, would you like to have me pose for my portrait?"

"Most willingly; and while you are posing, you can tell me something of your aerial experiences; you must have had a lot of them, and some very interesting."

"Well, you can judge that yourself. Tomorrow at nine o'clock, after early breakfast. If that is all right, I am going to bed now."

"That will be splendid. Captain, I am going too."

CHAPTER 18

Guynemer

The following day the weather changed and it was raining. "All the better," I thought, "Guynemer will not be tempted to go out." And so indeed, when I entered the dining-room, he was already there.

"Bad weather. Captain," I said.

"It's funny," he replied; "I can't get used to being called that, and I really prefer they should go on calling me 'kid'; a title like Captain makes me feel too old."

"How can you help it?" said I. "War makes young captains, and I know your relatives and friends don't agree with you."

"My two sisters are particularly pleased, though I can't say they are happy, for whenever I leave them, I can see they are afraid they will never see me again."

"Well, now, if you're ready, we will begin. Would you prefer that we go to your room?"

"Yes, I think I should; I have already started a good fire in there with wood that doesn't smoke. I collected it from pieces of Boche air propellers."

"Phew, what sacrilege!"

"Why so? Do you want any of it?"

"Well, I wouldn't say no if you asked me."

"All right, I will send you some very interesting pieces. You have never been in my home in Compiègne. I have already started a very good war museum there: about twenty machine guns, airplanes that I have brought down, and all sorts of things—eve-

A victory of Guynemer's

rything except the scientific instruments, which I am required to send to the technical section for examination. When an enemy machine falls near them, the *poilus* always get there before me. The scoundrels simply pick it to pieces; five minutes later it is like a plucked fowl, there is nothing left but the bones. How is the portrait coming along?"

"I will show it to you in a moment. I am very much afraid that you will take time from your war work for this simple peace work."

"Well, we will do both together."

"How can you manage that?" I asked.

"Bechereau made a most extraordinary photographic apparatus for me; it is secured to the machine gun, and it operates at the same time as the gun. You know very well I have brought down a great many Boches over our lines that have not been counted. Now with my snapshot Kodak, there will be no more doubts; no one can contest a photograph. I am crazy to try it."

"It is certainly a sure proof for everybody, and valuable, for it must be exasperating beyond words to see an adversary fall in flames and not be able to count him among one's victories."

"Yes; and then it is disgusting to have to go to look for them as far as their camps, for the farther we go, the less these gentlemen Boches will come up to our lines, or when they do come, they come in groups of three and four at a time."

"Your fights must be very much alike, but the end, I suppose, is very different."

"Well, yes and no. I have in mind three fights—all victories, which bear no resemblance to each other. Every fight is more or less governed by the kind of machine one is fighting. If it is a fighting plane—that is, a monoplane like our Spad—it is a real fight of about equal force and skill, and in such a case, the comparative skill of the pilots is what determines the fight; but of course there is always a strong element of luck. Accuracy of aim at the speed at which we fight (about 160 kilometres an hour) is a very difficult thing. When you think that should you pass a centimetre's breadth either to the right or to the left, you are a dead man, it must be admitted that luck counts for a good deal. How many times I came near being killed either by bullets or by shrapnel, which have gone through my clothes! But at the time I never gave it a thought.

"Now if we attack a biplane, it is a different kind of a fight; a bi-plane can only take the defensive, and very badly at that. When I say that, I have in mind our poor old Farman and Voisin machines; they have the propeller in the rear. That is a splendid protection for the Boche fighting planes, or any others, in fact. It is only necessary for them to have a little more speed, and they will then be able to take position where and when they please, and bring down the foe easily without receiving any punishment."

"Well," I said, thinking of Navarre when he flew all around me over Verdun, "the Boche planes are sometimes hampered by that inferiority."

"It is much more difficult to bring down their observation planes than for them to bring down ours, just on account of this: their dead angle is more limited. Poor unfortunate observation comrades—it is all right—I have well avenged some of you. I am always seeing in my mind's eye that Rumpler turning end-over-end, a mass of flames plunging through a sea of clouds like a mad thing, and the sun lighting it up with its bright morning beams thrown across the battle-ground.

"The Boche machine was set aflame by gun-fire and was tumbling in somersaults. I could see that as soon as the pilot was shot, his wound caused him to make mistakes in the management of the plane, and that the lifebelts which held the two passengers secure were both cut by gun-fire, throwing both of the occupants out of the machine; they disappeared through space and into the banks of clouds. Only a trail of smoke, leading through the pure white clouds, showed that the machine had ever been.

"I should have been sad, indeed, if I had not descended to deliver an unfortunate Farman returning from some spotting work, for if I had not got to him when I did, he would surely have met the same fate.

"My second adventure was very much like the first, except that I just missed having the observer fall on top of me; it was in trying to save one of our planes. Although I brought him down at the first shot, I recognized that I had to deal with a good marksman with plenty of spirit and *sang-froid*. He fired regularly, slowly, and carefully, and I noticed that he took his time; that he aimed carefully, for his bullets whistled past my ears uncomfortably close, several going through my clothes and one through my cap. I heard their noise above that of the motor. 'Lord!' thought I, 'if I don't get into his dead angle, he will surely get me.'

"The pilot must have been very experienced, for he managed his machine beautifully, and materially assisted his machine-gunner by his careful turns, constantly giving him the advantage. I slowed down in order not to draw away, and placed myself a little below him. I had not yet fired, in spite of about twenty shots that I had received, but when I secured a position of advantage, I touched off a whole string of cartridges. I noted that the bullets—some of them—reached the target, and that the pilot must have been killed, for in the last fall he gave the tiller a fierce throwover, so that the machine tumbled suddenly and threw the observer into the air; as I was flying directly behind him, I had to make a sudden swerve to avoid catching his body on my wings. I can see him still with his arms thrown out into the air, remaining just a second as if suspended from heaven, and then shooting down into space."

"That is very interesting, indeed," said I, interrupting.

"Ah, but my third is the finest; I believe it to be unique in the whole history of aviation. It gave me my most cherished citation, which was from my comrades of the '*cigognes*.' It was not really official."

"And that is what makes it all the more precious, isn't it?"

"My word, yes; and that's the one I want to tell you about. I was trying out a new machine, and not expecting to fight, I had not loaded my gun according to my usual habit. I flew over the line and I was going along peacefully, not dreaming of harm, when all at once I was attacked by an Albatross biplane. I opened up the motor and got away from him by zigzagging, watching carefully for a chance to turn around. Finally, after a half-turn, I saw him draw away from me. 'All right,' I said to myself, 'if he is trying to get away, what can be the matter with him? Is his machine gun jammed? Hasn't he any more cartridges? That may be.'

"I determined to make out what the trouble was, at all hazards. 'I will creep up on him,' thought I, 'and if he doesn't fire, it is because he can't.'

"I plunged down a little, in order to increase my speed, and in two minutes I was underneath him, and got him within my arc of fire. The fear of being brought down terrified him so that his gunner threw his arms up and made a sign of *Kamerad*. I did the same as a sign of recognition and consent, and with my arm I indicated the direction to steer. Easily and quietly I piloted him back to our own camp.

"It would be impossible to describe to you the astonishment of the mechanics at seeing a Boche plane coming voluntarily into their midst, with me following. As soon as I got to the ground, I jumped out and went up to my captive and presented myself, 'Lieutenant Guynemer!' His face brightened up with a kind of pride; he was quite satisfied to be captured by me.

"'Well,' said I, 'you were wrong to give yourself up, for I didn't have a single shot in my gun.' Ah, if you could have seen his face change expression; it was certainly comical. Enraged, the observer, without our noticing, pressed an electric button which set fire to his gasoline tank and burnt up the machine. It was I then who no longer laughed, for I was so happy to have captured that Boche plane, as it was an entirely new one.

"It seems that I had a fierce look, with a mouth like an assassin. My photograph was taken at the time, and here it is. Look at that face!"

"Oh, that's splendid; I'd like to have it and also a drawing of those three victories."

"So would I, although I can draw about as much as a stone

can swim. How's my portrait getting along?"

"The head is finished—here it is; for the uniform I will pose your orderly, if that is agreeable, and it will require only one more sitting."

"All right; if this weather continues tomorrow, we will have another sitting. Do you know that you are the first whoever succeeded in doing anything with me, although it is true that I have hardly had time to pose? My family will be delighted with this, and it is perfectly astonishing how rapidly you have done it."

"Oh, that's all right; I have a very strong incentive. I can do a lot of painting in an hour."

"Look here, that expression isn't bad."

"I say, kid," cried the sharp voice of Captain Auger, "you don't want to fly today, do you?"

"Yes, what time is it?—half-past twelve! The Commandant will be angry. It seems to me that there are a good many vacancies today. Where are de la Tour, Dorme, Duval?" asked Guynemer, sitting down.

"You are very indiscreet, my dear Captain Guynemer," said Heurtaux calmly; "and *apropos*, is Duval going to leave us?"

"Yes, they have prohibited photographic service in fighting groups," answered the commandant. "I am certainly astonished at it, for it was the best of all. Here's a man recovered from his wounds received in the trenches, who might remain at home; he prefers to continue active service; he doesn't want to leave us, but I can see only one way to accommodate him, and that is after he has passed his examination. After that I will see what can be done to get him a job as pilot in number three."

"Oh, yes," said Heurtaux, "it is truly astonishing, I think, and we shall be only too happy to have him; isn't that right, everybody?"

"That's quite right. Tell him to make his request, will you, Heurtaux?"

"I will, with pleasure."

"Well, Farré, how 's everything with you?"

"Not bad. Commandant, I am working on Guynemer."

ANOTHER VICTORY OF GUYNEMER'S

"Since you completed Auger, Deullin, Dorme, I am not worrying anymore."

"Under your care. Commandant, it couldn't be otherwise."

"What bad weather it is today; one would think that we were at Cachy on the Somme."

"Yes; the weather was very much the same that time I came to see you. Commandant, tell me your feeling about those little personal trips which you loved to make in returning from expeditions?"

"I don't get you."

"I was over Chaulnes with Captain de Kerillis, and you passed so close to me that I read the number of your plane. 'Ah,' said de Kerillis, 'there is Brocard at his old game; he is going to fly low and have some fun with the Boche cantonments in Chaulnes.'"

"Ah, I liked that sector. What fine work we did! We brought down so many Boches that we were truly masters of the air. I certainly enjoyed that. What would you do? I soon ceased to find game in the air, so went hunting on the earth—there 's fine hunting there. One day in the main street of Chaulnes, I began racing an automobile filled with a lot of officers. I must have petrified the chauffeur, because after a wild flight across the city, he dashed into an artillery train, which was going our way. You can imagine the result. Add to that the fire I kept up with my machine gun, and you have a very pretty picture of war. I never regretted my little detour on that occasion, for lacking anything better, I had eaten sparrows, which I found very good after all. It is the last resource of the unfortunate hunter; not wishing to bring back any cartridges, he fires them off at any old enemy and leaves them as his visiting card.

"When there's a chance to surprise the relief for the trenches, that is more dangerous, for then there are machine guns against airplanes."

"Commandant."

"What was the matter, my boy?"

"Did you notice this morning the face of the Captain who came to call on you with the Staff?"

"Yes, but what was the matter with it?"

"Oh, it was rich. Before coming to your office, they stopped at the field, and I was sitting calmly on the edge of my plane in overalls, smoking a cigarette. My rank marks were invisible, and on coming near me, he said, 'Tell me, my little friend—'"

"That doesn't surprise me—you look so young," interrupted the commandant.

"He said, 'Is this the famous Stork Escadrille?'

"'Yes, Captain,' I replied.

"'Well, where are the aces? I don't see one.'

"'Ah, Captain, you know,' I said to him in my gayest manner, 'that's something one doesn't see every day. When they are not flying, they are seldom at the field, and when it rains as it does today, they stay in bed, like the lazy rascals they are. It is difficult, indeed, for you to see one.' He did not seem to be satisfied with that. I had some fun at his expense without knowing who he was, and when you presented me to the General—Lieutenant Heurtaux, Commandant of the Stork Escadrille—the Captain who was the Staff officer recognized me in spite of my change of dress, but I never let on. Nevertheless, he knew me as the mechanic who had fun with him in the morning."

"Always the cap and bells," said the commandant; "you are never serious."

"Well, it 's all right if we can bring down the Boches, isn't it. Auger?"

"You disgust me, sir; I don't want to serve under you. I was ashamed the other day when the Minister and General of Infantry passed us in review. Didn't you find it exasperating to see that kid Heurtaux with his two stripes; and what did the General say?"

"He asked me first who was the Commandant of the Escadrille.

"'Lieutenant Heurtaux, General.'

"'Commandant, I don't understand,' he answered. 'I see eight officers, three captains, and Lieutenant Heurtaux commands them. Is he a captain?'

"Just then Heurtaux came up to us, saying his third stripe would come very soon.

"'That would be absurd; the Stork Escadrille will soon be a Captain Escadrille.'

"Why not, as long as I remain your Commandant?" We were finishing our lunch.

"This coffee is rotten, don't you think so? In order to lighten up the gloom, I will play you a little bit of Beethoven."

"Don't you think he is nice and honest?" said the commandant. "He is just like a sweet young lady; look at that bland smile and that innocent expression. Unfortunately he is not entirely lucky. He always comes out of his fights knocked up in some way, for he has had three wounds and that is what annoys him so. He has twenty-one Boche planes to his credit, and he would have doubled that record had he not spent so much time in the hospital."

Whenever the mail arrives, it brings a feeling of gayety and humour, and the postman is certainly a very welcome fellow. Guynemer is always the favourite. For a quarter of an hour there is very little said; the family letters are read first, and then the others; there is no conversation. At two o'clock they all break up; those who have military duties go to work at them. The others read, waiting for the weather to improve, so that they can spread their wings and fly off into the blue in search of new victories.

A rainy afternoon is spent generally after the following manner. Very much like the birds that seem to be mortally afraid of wetting their feathers and remain in their retreats thoughtful and quiet, fighting aviators follow the same plan, and prefer to remain in their quarters in their slippers, reading before a good fire whenever they can have one. Sometimes, but not often, they play cards.

After about four weeks of this kind of life, I left the Stork Escadrille with a series of portraits and sketches of all descriptions. I was going to finish these various studies later on, and accompany them with stories told by the heroes themselves, adding to them my own personal experiences, so as to make them as near the truth as possible. I could not finish the portrait of Guynemer, who was called to Paris to inspect a new plane for which he designed the armament.

"I am leaving for Paris," he said to me in reply to my request to give him one more sitting, "to test out the armament of my 'new *coucou.*' I am going to carry a thirty-seven, which will fire through the propeller. Old man, it is a regular marvel, and you can just see me bring down the Boches with it."

"You certainly are a wonder; not satisfied with bringing them down, you are devoting yourself to perfecting your gun."

"Yes; God knows I had trouble enough to get it adopted by the technical section, but it is all right at last, and I will try it out next week. Are you returning to Paris soon?"

"In two or three days, I hope."

"All right, come and look me up at the Hotel Edward VII, and we will arrange a date for our portrait."

A few days afterward I took leave of Commandant Brocard and my new friends, and leaving Manoncourt, I returned to Paris to turn over my new paintings to General Niox, director of the Army Museum. As soon as I arrived I left word at the Hotel Edward VII for Guynemer. The next day he came to my studio, and I was able at last to get him for a whole hour entirely at my disposal, but even that time was not sufficient to allow me to get his fine face as I wanted it. I thought, "I will have time later on to finish it up," but, alas, I was mistaken. Fate decreed otherwise, for he soon became immortal in the full glory of his career.

"Shall we have luncheon together, Guynemer?" I asked him.

"Certainly, thank you."

"And afterwards, another little pose?"

"Ah, no, my friend, I have got to be at Buc at three o'clock and try out my new gun, and since it is dark at five o'clock, it will be necessary for us to hurry up luncheon, but I will promise to give you another sitting before I leave for the front. Would you like to come along and witness the trying out of my new gun?"

"With the greatest of pleasure!"

"We will take luncheon somewhere on the Grand Boulevard, and in that way we shall lose less time in getting to Buc."

They had a one-hundred horse-power Hispano Suiza racing-car, a big white car with the engine snorting outside like thunder. We ran rapidly down the Rue Pigalle. After lunch we climbed into its comfortable *tonneau*, and noticed pinned on our steering-wheel a square sheet of white paper, upon which was written, *Sale embusqué* (You slacker).

"Can you beat it?" he asked, laughing.

"Does that happen to you often?"

"Sometimes, but not often. Once I found the car full of flowers; another time full of women's old hats. It all depends upon whether I am known or not. When I wear my cloak, they take me for a slacker; when I don't wear it, I get flowers.

"One day I was with Heurtaux. We went directly to Buc, and having a little trouble with the machine, we stopped there. In the meantime we were passed by another automobile carrying two persons, who, seeing us laughing and behaving like kids, shouted 'Slackers!' to us as they went by.

"I said to Heurtaux, 'Look here, let's teach those devils a lesson.'

"'All right,' said he; 'that's what we've got to do.' We shot ahead like a cannon ball, and the big white automobile took up the chase of the wretches who had shouted at us.

"Finally we passed them, turned around, and blocked the way. They had to stop, visibly surprised. I jumped out and climbed up on their running-board and said, 'Which of you two called us slackers?'

"'I did,' said one of them in an arrogant tone. 'All right, my son, I am Captain Guynemer and this is Captain Heurtaux,'— and throwing back our cloaks, we showed them our uniforms. Seeing our decorations, they turned white; at the same time a slap in the face from me started the fellow stammering out some excuses. Both Heurtaux and myself were very much amused."

"Look here, it seems to me that we are going at an unusual speed through the streets of Paris," I said, as we flew along, making turns which, without fine control, would have turned out badly indeed for us.

"The police know me; and besides, we are not out for our health alone. It is twenty kilometres from here to Buc, and we have to be there in about twenty minutes; five minutes afterwards I must be in the air—so the good people of Paris will have to stand it."

"You are always in the war zone."

"Absolutely."

We crossed Versailles in a cloud of dust, and three minutes afterwards we arrived at Buc. The sentry on duty presented arms, and everything was ready for the experiment. All the personnel of the school was out paying their tribute of admiration to the young hero. Small balloons larger than a man's head were sent up in the air. As soon as they were high enough, Guynemer shot up after them and brought them down with his gun.

I heard his first shot as he attacked this inoffensive enemy. At that shot the balloon burst, the second the same way; then Guynemer came down saying that he couldn't keep it up—something had gone wrong with the gun. "Something blew out of the breech and just passed my face; but that's a little detail," he said, "and experience teaches us a lot." In all his talks he was short and exact and never used superfluous words.

"I want to take you back home. Is that agreeable?"

"Shall we have the evening together?"

"No, not this evening; I am flying across Paris to see my family in Compiègne, where they are waiting for me; and for you, too, for they want to know you. The day after tomorrow, the Commandant and Heurtaux will be there and we shall dine together; the Commandant and I have something to talk over. Will you come?"

"All right, then, the day after tomorrow at the Café de la Paix at seven o'clock."

Two days later found me at the rendezvous, and Commandant Brocard, who was then in Paris on a special mission of twenty-four hours, joined us there.

"We are going to dine at the house of ——."

"Yes, all right. Commandant, I have had a telephone call from the lady. She has never forgotten Mouchard, and when I think of her, there is ever present before me the recollection of that dear friend looking at her photograph, for she is a truly beautiful and accomplished woman."

"She has just received her second prize, did you know it?"

"No, but it doesn't astonish me. Ah, here's the kid himself. Let's go. Heurtaux will join us at her house; he knows her address."

We got into Guynemer's machine, and ten minutes later we were there. We spent a most enjoyable evening, which I feel it would be indiscreet for me to describe, and at which Guynemer was at his best. The next day the commandant left Paris and returned to his head-quarters.

"And you, you kid," said the commandant; "did you finish your experiments?"

"Yes, Commandant, and I shall remain for forty-eight hours longer if the bad weather lasts, but if it clears up I shall come back immediately. I am getting homesick for the Boche." Seeing the expression on my face, he added, "Don't be worried, Farré; come and get me at the hotel tomorrow at nine o'clock; I will leave word there for you. I shall not go away without posing for you once more."

Alas! I was never to see him again. The next day he was recalled by telephone. Eight days later, as I was coming out of the office of the Minister of War, I learned that, after a sortie made by Guynemer in company with one of his comrades of the *Escadrille,* he failed to return. The 11th of September, 1917, was the last day of his stay in this world. He had gone out in reconnaissance about nine o'clock in the morning.

I heard directly from Lieutenant Bozon-Verduraz, who was with him when he disappeared. Guynemer saw an enemy machine, and following his accustomed habit, he flew straight for it. All at once several hostile planes rose out of the clouds and came to the rescue of their comrade.

"Realizing the risk he was running," said Lieutenant Bozon-Verduraz, "I myself attacked the new arrivals and succeeded in dispersing them. I then turned around and looked for my dear comrade. Alas! In all the immensity of that sea of clouds, I could see no trace of Guynemer; his plane had disappeared."

Tales of prisoners give various accounts of his death, but they are not official, and it still remains shrouded in mystery. It would seem that the glory of the skies had been jealous of the glory of the earth, and had snatched up our hero into the ether—called him as Elijah was called in a chariot of fire—and the earth, that knew him once throughout its length and breadth, shall know him no more forever.

Guynemer might have remained quietly at home, where he was coddled and loved, but his high sense of duty and his love of country impelled him ever to new achievement. With him it required almost as much courage to combat the hostility of the recruiting officers as to fight the enemy. Once at Compiègne, where he lived with his family, and twice at Bayonne, he asked the approval of his family to enter the service; but was always rejected by the recruiting officers on account of his delicate and frail appearance. Nothing daunted by these rebuffs, he tried again and again.

Provided with a letter of introduction to Captain Bernard Thierry, commanding the aviation school at Pau, he begged him to take him on.

"Take me, Captain; I will do anything that you ask me to do," he said.

"Do you want to be a mechanic?" said the captain. "That is all I can offer you, but if you want that, you must lose no time about it; you can come right away."

"I am not a mechanic yet, Captain, but if you will kindly give me a word of introduction to the recruiting officer and say that I am capable of doing the duties you designate, you will assist me very much in being accepted."

"All right, I will be glad to do so; I will give you a word to take along with you, and I hope soon to congratulate you upon your being taken on."

George Guynemer was at last enlisted on November 23, 1914, as a volunteer for the duration of the war. His desire to serve his country in spite of every obstacle was at last realized, and he became a soldier. He led a rough life at the aviation school at Pau; he did all the chores and hard work around the place, but did everything with absolute delight. He was an apprentice mechanic, and he loved mechanics.

"What more could I wish?" he said; "a mechanic's job may lead to anything if one only knows how to go about it."

Finally he passed the examination for pilot and was accepted. On January 25, 1915, he became a pilot, and on June 8 he was detailed to the Stork Escadrille; on July 20 he was promoted to the rank of sergeant. On the 23rd of the same month he was awarded the Military Medal with his first citation.

On the day he reached his majority, December 24, 1915,—for he was born on Christmas Eve,—he was made Chevalier of the Legion of Honour, and got his stripe as sub-lieutenant on March 4, 1916. On the 18th of February following, when he was twenty-two years old, he was made a captain, and on the 25th of May of that year, he surpassed all his previous exploits by bringing down four Boche planes in one day.

About August 30, 1917, his record showed fifty-three planes brought down, twenty-seven citations in general order, and two wounds; besides, the number of his victories greatly exceeded the total of those officially confirmed—nearly a hundred, he told me one day while he was posing.

The city of Compiègne did honour to the memory of its son in a splendid and imposing service conducted by the Bishop at the cathedral, where representatives of the army and of the Government were present. After this ceremony—in company with Captain Heurtaux, who was convalescing from a new wound, and Lieutenant Raymond—I paid a visit to the family of Guynemer.

George Guynemer was adored by his family, his parents and two sisters, and he was equally fond of them. He looked very much like his father, and although somewhat larger, he resembled him in his grace and slenderness of figure. He inherited his air of distinction from his mother.

"You see," said Monsieur Guynemer, his father, showing me a large pile of letters received from the four quarters of the earth, "why I have not replied to yours. My wife and daughters beg you will excuse them; they are completely prostrated; the ceremony has over-whelmed them, but they hope to be down presently." A deep sadness showed in his face; a dignified grief, intense but resigned, was portrayed in his drawn features.

"We all felt," he went on, "when he left the last time, that he would never come back. We did not dare mention our fears—it was only afterwards that we talked about it, and expressed our feelings regarding his return. We think he must have had the same *presentiment*, because when he was leaving us, he did not appear as composed as usual. Dear boy, in spite of the war and what he passed through, he was still the same sweet child. Just before leaving he reproached his sisters for forgetting him, and charged them with not having prepared his room properly the night before. 'You are neglecting me, young ladies,' he said. At home, whenever he went to bed, his sisters never failed to go and bid him goodnight."

"Monsieur Guynemer," I said, "I think you have on your desk a reproduction of the portrait I made of your son. You must like it."

"Oh, extremely so, and I do not mean to flatter you when I assure you that it is the best that was ever made of him."

"Will you join me in undertaking a good work. Monsieur Guynemer?"

"Very willingly, sir; what must I do?"

"It is this. I am leaving in about three weeks for America, to show our allies over there what French aviation has done during the war. I have authority and permission from the Government to exhibit my pictures in every city in the United States; and naturally I shall carry with me the portrait of your son. I want to sell copies of it for the benefit of aviation. Will you kindly autograph some of these as a souvenir of him?"

"I shall be most happy to do so—but not today."

"Of course not, and it wouldn't be possible today, for I haven't made the pictures yet."

"All right—next week, perhaps. Telegraph me twenty-four hours in advance of the hour of your coming, and I will be at home and alone, and you can take luncheon with me. Afterwards I will sign everything you want. I would like to add some of his souvenirs of the war, but we haven't yet had the courage to go into his room. Whenever he flew over Compiègne, he used to love to come down and just graze the roof of our house, so as to terrify his mother and sisters."

His father told me many anecdotes of him, and was often forced to stop, overcome with emotion; so this natural feeling prevented his keeping up continued conversation, but he did justice to the facts as he told them.

"Don't you find comfort in your bereavement. Monsieur Guynemer, by the way all the world offers its homage to the heroism of your son?" I asked him.

Shaking his head sadly, and lifting his eyes to heaven, he said, "I would rather have my child."

"Have you received any real official information?"

"None whatever—everything is mystery. The King of Spain himself sent me word that no reply had been made to his request" (for news of Guynemer) .

On the occasion of the last citation of Guynemer, which was the 26th, one given after his disappearance, the famous Stork Escadrille No. 3 was assembled on a beautiful day, shortly after the announcement of his death, to listen to a solemn reading of the last and sublime homage that the army offered their great hero who had disappeared in the heights of the air and left no trace. Of dear friends whom I had known at Manoncourt and who had flown away and disappeared, Guynemer was the fourth.

Captain Duval, photographic observer, had passed his examination for pilot with the full intention of remaining with his friends, the Storks, but unfortunately he was not present on the field at this time. Right here I ought to give an account of his service, and show how his high sense of duty and devotion to his country aided him to accomplish more than was demanded by simple routine service.

While an infantryman, he was wounded in the trenches, and almost lost one leg, but would not accept his retirement to the rear. He insisted upon doing duty as photographic observer in aviation. Attached to Escadrille No. 3, he was shortly afterwards dismissed, owing to the suppression of photography in fighting *escadrilles*; so that, in order not to leave his friends, and in spite of his shortened leg, he became a pilot and remained with them.

Not being appointed to take any special part in the ceremony, he requested permission of the commandant to fly over the aviation field during the reading of the citation.

"It will be a deep and sincere pleasure to me," he said, "and it will be symbolic and render visible—so to speak—the soul of Guynemer, who without doubt will be with us at that time."

All the planes were drawn up in a sort of square on the aviation field, with all the pilots of the fighting group in the centre. Standing by their planes, they formed a small square, in the centre of which the commandant placed himself, and facing the pilots, he said with an unsteady voice, "Trumpeters, sound colours."

At the conclusion of the call, with a voice that he did his best to command, he recited a resume of the great qualities and exploits of the absent comrade, and concluded by reading the Posthumous Citation, which ran as follows:

Fallen on the field of honour on September 11, 1917. A legendary hero, fallen from the very zenith of Victory after three years' hard and continuous fighting. He will be considered the most perfect embodiment of the national qualities for his indomitable energy and perseverance and his exalted gallantry. Full of invincible belief in Victory, he has bequeathed to the French soldier an imperishable memory, which must add to his self-sacrificing spirit and will surely give rise to the noblest emulation.

Captain Henry Duval flew over the aviation field at about two hundred meters; in the middle of this solemn reading he was seen to lose control of his plane. His machine veered suddenly on one wing. Too near the ground to execute the manoeuvre required to re-establish his equilibrium, we saw him fall heavily and crash to earth. A horrible moment! Everyone was stirred by that unfortunate accident, but not a pilot moved or even looked; they stood like statues of bronze. Only the commandant stopped his reading, and, turning toward the unfortunate Duval, made him a military salute.

Wonderful and tragic scene! A human sacrifice that only the patriotic love of country could render possible. Everybody not in ranks immediately ran towards the new dead hero, killed in falling; his soul had risen to join that of Guynemer, to heighten by example the courage of their comrades, to whom they left the task in which they themselves could no longer share.

LEONAUR

ALSO FROM LEONAUR
AVAILABLE IN SOFTCOVER OR HARDCOVER WITH DUST JACKET

ARMOURED CARS IN EDEN *by K. Roosevelt*—An American President's son serving in Rolls Royce armoured cars with the British in Mesopatamia & with the American Artillery in France during the First World War.

CHASSEUR OF 1914 by *Marcel Dupont*—Experiences of the twilight of the French Light Cavalry by a young officer during the early battles of the great war in Europe.

TROOP HORSE & TRENCH by *R.A. Lloyd*—The experiences of a British Life-guardsman of the household cavalry fighting on the western front during the First World War 1914-18.

THE LONG PATROL by *George Berrie*—A Novel of Light Horsemen from Gallipoli to the Palestine campaign of the First World War.

THE EAST AFRICAN MOUNTED RIFLES *by C.J. Wilson*—Experiences of the campaign in the East African bush during the First World War

THE FIGHTING CAMELIERS *by Frank Reid*—The exploits of the Imperial Camel Corps in the desert and Palestine campaigns of the First World War.

WITH THE IMPERIAL CAMEL CORPS IN THE GREAT WAR by *Geoffrey Inchbald*—The story of a serving officer with the British 2nd battalion against the Senussi and during the Palestine campaign.

STEEL CHARIOTS IN THE DESERT by *S.C.Rolls*—The first world war experiences of a Rolls Royce armoured car driver with the Duke of Westminster in Libya and in Arabia with T.E. Lawrence.

INFANTRY BRIGADE: 1914 by *Edward Gleichen*—The Diary of a Commander of the 15th Infantry Brigade, 5th Division, British Army, During the Retreat from Mons

HEARTS & DRAGONS by *Charles R. M. F. Crutwell*—The 4th Royal Berkshire Regiment in France and Italy During the Great War, 1914-1918.

TIGERS ALONG THE TIGRIS by *E. J. Thompson*—The Leicestershire Regiment in Mesopotamia During the First World War.

DESPATCH RIDER by *W. H. L. Watson*—The Experiences of a British Army Motorcycle Despatch Rider During the Opening Battles of the Great War in Europe.

www.ingramcontent.com/pod-product-compliance
Lightning Source LLC
Chambersburg PA
CBHW021106090426
42738CB00006B/519